To MELLY

LoVE
TREV
2020 X

1

Still Rolling;
A life of possibility not disability

By Tony Trev Baker

Dedicated to my dad, who has been there for me
through thick and thin, and without his love and
support, half of this adventure wouldn't have been
possible and life could have been very difficult.

*"Yesterday is history, tomorrow is a mystery, and
today is a gift that's why it's the present!"*

Cover design by Russell Gardner

www.liferollson.co.uk

ISBN 9781091542921

Testimonials

"Trev is resilience personified! A rolling inspiration, author, accomplished public speaker and action man. The term post traumatic growth is a reflection of Trev's life after suffering a catastrophic life changing injury that left him paralysed. This event was a catalyst that eventually saw Trevor go from an able bodied person with a love of the outdoors to what many would say is the best version of himself and the proud holder of a BA degree. This is reflected in his journey and talks. Trevor's unique combination of humour, brutal honesty, humility and charisma makes him a world class speaker, author and motivational coach."
Reece Coker Founder SquarePeg

"A remarkable story from someone with such severe disabilities following an accident.
This should serve as an inspiration to those with similar disabilities."
M Tasker

"We could all learn a lot from Trev.
 While most people don't really have a lot to complain about in life, many are very good at searching and

searching until they find something to whinge and whine about.

In all of the time the I've known Trev it's very rare to hear him complain about anything (he does sometimes of course, he's human like the rest of us) There are many things that we take for granted, walking, feeding ourselves and never give them a second thought. So how is it that a man who's life was changed, literally in a flash, and lost things that we consider to be so fundamental to our existence, can be so matter of fact about it?

Simply put it's in his attitude to life. I haven't yet figured out exactly what it is but its' got to be something like "Ok life - you can knock me down as many times as you want to, but I won't stay down! If you knock me down 7 times I'll get up 7 times" And he's good at it. When he tells me stories of some of the challenges he's faced I find my self wondering how he manages to carry on and even laugh about it. I have the privilege of knowing him as a friend and having worked with him too. Most of you won't have the pleasure of actually getting to know him but you can do the next best thing, read his books and get to see him speak if you can.

We could all learn a lot from Trev and we'd be short-changing ourselves if we didn't. "

Tony Leake Positive Changes August 2018

'I have seen Trev deliver his story a number of times now and each time it inspires me more and more. Listening to Trev talk about his experiences is truly motivational and makes me determined to achieve more with my life. Trev's book is a must read too. I highly recommend booking Trev if you are looking for a speaker to inspire and build resilience.'
Sharon Bartlett MJB Consultancy

About Life Rolls On; The journey from an AB to BA. "This book is an education to all of us, especially those who have never experienced severe disability. Mr. Baker is an inspiration. His book is easy to read and extremely interesting, narrating in brave and lucid detail his physical, mental and emotional experience during his journey from being fit and extremely active, through the terrible fall that robbed him of most of his movement, to his graduation as a Bachelor of Arts. Written as it is in a matter-of-fact rather than a self-pitying tone, this book is not harrowing as it might have been, but gripping and informative. Well done to Mr. Baker. I look forward to his next book, "From B.A. to ....."
J Radford (B.A) Humanistic Counseling

CONTENTS

Introduction

My name is Tony Trev Baker, and I live in a town called Retford in Nottinghamshire. I prefer to be called Trev. I am a C4 Tetraplegic, which means I broke my neck, four vertebrae from the top, this happened on New Year's Eve in 1999. I use a powerchair for mobility, and I live independently with 24-hour care.

I previously wrote and published a book in 2012, about my injury and my recovery. This tells the story about my accident, going skiing, moving home. The start of my studies in sports coaching and eventually rolling across a stage to become a Bachelor of Arts graduate.

My first book, which is called Life Rolls On, The Journey from an AB to a BA. Available at www.liferollson.co.uk.

This book is an autobiography, I hope that others will take inspiration from my own experiences and be able to implement changes into their own lives.

1
S.A.N.D. (SEE ABILITY NOT DISABILITY)

The S.A.N.D. Sports Club (See Ability Not Disability) is a sports club for children with disabilities that I have a great passion for. I initially got involved in 2001 as part of my placement for the Community Sports Leader Award, I had to do ten voluntary hours to gain my qualification. I am still involved and will continue applying my passion to this initiative.

We are always innovating at the S.A.N.D. sports club and are constantly trying to give the children new experiences as well as always challenging ourselves as leaders.

We booked an activity weekend in the Yorkshire Dales, which is one of my favourite places in the U.K. This weekend was paid for through some fundraising that we had done previously, and the parents only had to pay a contribution towards it.

The accommodation was fantastic and well equipped for everyone including myself. I had a two-bedroom suite with an adjustable bed and an overhead tracking hoist that enabled me to go from the bed, straight into the shower and toilet.

For some of the children it would have been the first time away from their families. It was excellent to see how they interacted with each other and how they coped being away from home.

Over the weekend it was admirable to see the children pushing themselves and having a great time. There were also some good challenges for me.

We participated in activities such as, abseiling, climbing, caving, zip lining and plenty of teamwork exercises. The centre had rigged up hoists made of a rope and pulley system in all the activity rooms. This made it easier to transfer from a wheelchair to the activity. I liked this idea, not only was every action accessible, it showed they had the initiative to adapt equipment using ropes, which helped build trust in the people and the facilities.

I was extremely excited about going caving, as I had never done it before. It was something, I never thought I would ever be able to experience, because I am a wheelchair user. We went down a cave called Yordas Cave in Kingsdale with the Bendrigg Trust Residential in North Yorkshire.

They had off-road wheelchairs that had large knobbly tires with an extra wheel at the front to enable steering.

I wasn't quite sure how we were going to go caving! They tied a rope to the front of my chair, and 2 or 3 people pulled me up the hill, which was quite funny and also quite scary. All the weight was at the back of the chair, which caused it to keep tipping over, and popping wheelies.

We were given a safety briefing before we went into the cave. I was lowered down in the chair along with two other wheelchair users, and then the rest of the group came down. It was a fantastic experience being underground in a cave, in the middle of the Yorkshire Dales, and seeing all of the old rock formations.

We were asked to turn off our head torches and sit in silence in complete darkness, which I liked, but the children didn't like too much. It was wonderful to watch the non-disabled children crawling around the many nooks and crannies and getting under the underwater falls. I had never been caving before, and it was something I never thought I would do, it was great fun!

Next on the agenda was going down a zip wire. I am a big believer in leading by example, so I was the first to go down the wire. I felt this showed my willingness to do it and that it was safe. It was an advantage to go first so I could sit at the bottom and encourage, reassure and motivate the children that it would be ok. If the zip wire could hold my 15 stone weight, it could easily cope with the weight of a child.

I was very nervous at the start of the zip wire. The staff put all the safety harnesses on me and made sure everything was secure, but it was still a little bit worrying seeing my feet dangling over the edge before being pushed off.

I loved whizzing down the zip wire and picking up more and more speed. It was the first time for me, and I enjoyed it. It was such fun! It was excellent to see the children having turns. A few of them were quite reluctant and anxious at the start, but they all enjoyed it and were glad to have had a go, most were asking to go again, but we didn't have time.

We then went onto the climbing wall where everyone got harnessed up and had a go at climbing. For some of them, it was the first time. All in all they did really well, and were all able to get up to the top, as there were different routes for different levels of ability.

They got me and the wheelchair users to go up a very steep incline which was quite scary but fun. The ropes were attached to a ratchet mechanism that helped pull the chair up the slope. I had to put my trust and faith into the equipment, as it started ascending, I just had to focus. It was a huge relief getting to the top, back on flat land. The important thing for me was seeing the members enjoying and pushing themselves. It was also good seeing them out of the club environment and interacting with each other and trying new activities.

The next residential was in the Peak District near Castleton. We only went for the weekend, and it was great fun. We travelled down on a Friday and arranged to meet people there as I went in my vehicle and everyone else travelled down in a minibus.

On arrival, we had an evening meal and a talk with the instructors to find out what we would be doing with the children. Usually, when we do residentials we split into 2 groups. I had a chat with the instructors in the morning, and we decided to keep everyone together.

The weather was lovely and dry, and the location was beautiful. We started with some team building exercises where the group had to hold hands and pass a hula-hoop over themselves. We then did this activity with two circles to make it more difficult.

The next exercise involved using sections of a drainpipe that was cut into different lengths and then cut in half. The idea was to get a golf ball, (which we pretended was an alien artefact) back to its origin. We began by getting everyone to make a continuous chain and rolling the ball down the drainpipes, the kids at the back had to go to the front to make sure the chain was unbroken. The origin was a tiny hole that the golf ball had to go through. We achieved this, but it did take several attempts, it was a great way of using hand-eye coordination and communication and was great fun!

We then did another activity where the children had to cross an imaginary fiery pit by using stepping-stones, which were square pieces of carpet. The person at the back had to pick up a stepping-stone and pass it along the line to the front, and then everyone stepped across. If two feet were not on a stepping-stone at any one time, then someone came in and took one away to make it more difficult.

We then spent a couple of hours on an assault course. Some of the children found this easy, and some of them struggled and had to push themselves to get over the obstacles. My role was to encourage and motivate the children to challenge themselves and get through the obstacles. I found it difficult to drive my chair around the obstacles, as the ground was rough and bumpy and not really wheelchair friendly.

The children also had to build rafts out of barrels, planks and ropes. They had to decide what would be the best design and approach. The children then had to follow instructions to get the best knots to hold the rafts together. We did boys versus girls. Once the floats were built, the children had to launch into the water and race around the small pond. Individual members had to perform specific tasks that involved getting on and off the raft, which was great for team building. It was awesome to watch the members having fun. It was one of the funniest things I had seen in a long time. The other volunteers and I couldn't stop laughing our heads off. They also learnt some bush craft skills such as, how to make a fire and how to make canopies. To finish off, they roasted marshmallows and made a hot drink from the fire they made.

We eventually split the group into 2. One Group went caving, and the other group did archery. I used an adapted bow that had been fixed onto a camera tripod, and the string was attached to a very delicate switch, which meant I was able to line up the bow and take some shots. I enjoyed archery. It was tricky lining up the bow because I had to instruct someone to line it up, by saying, "left a bit, right a bit, up a bit". Once I had it lined up, I found it reasonably accurate and got in some good shots.

We did plenty more teamwork games. It was an excellent weekend for the club. The children's communication skills were vastly improved, and they learnt different skills, improved teamwork and had great fun.

I found out on the weekend that one of the organisers had tried to get some funding to cover the weekend, but this had been rejected, so the parents had to pay. However, someone had seen the rejection application and decided that what we were doing for the children with disabilities was amazing and decided to give an anonymous donation of £3300. This was fantastic, because this meant that parents got their money back.

I never found out who had made this generous donation that enabled the children to have such a great experience and adventure. The only thing that he asked for was to see some evidence that his money had been used well. I took my video camera, and we filmed quite a lot of footage over the weekend. When I got home, I edited the footage and created an excellent DVD.

The DVD was also good for the parents, as the children often tell their parents what they do, but they never get to see anything. All the parents said it was beautiful and so nice to be able to have a DVD showing what fun and what activities they had done. What an excellent keepsake to look back on in future years too!

It's been fascinating over the years, watching young children come to the club and then progress into college. The club has an age limit of 18, but a lot of them will stay on, as there is nowhere else for them to go. It has been interesting the last couple of years, I've been invited to 18th and 21st birthday parties, heard stories about their experiences growing up, driving lessons, getting boyfriends and girlfriends. Life rolls on for everyone.

We ran a dance session throughout the club every Monday night for ten weeks. Some of the children embraced this and some of them didn't, but I felt that they were missing out on sports sessions. We had a specialist dance instructor come in to work with them.

She structured the movements around sport to keep with the theme of the club. It was great when they put on a show for family and friends to demonstrate what they had learnt. The instructor got funding to put on a separate dance class for a more extended period that meant, those who wanted to take it more seriously could and so, this became Sandance. This meant that the sports club could continue to be a sports club.

I had nothing to do with this, but it was great when they put on a show at the end of the term, along with ten other dance groups from various schools. I had no idea what they were going to do, and I was amazed at the performance they put on and how their timing and confidence had dramatically increased. What a great feeling to know that someone else had coached and nurtured them so they could produce an outstanding show.

We are fundamentally a sports club. However, it is much more than that, as we try to offer the children many different experiences. We would not be able to run as a club without Sian's dedication and Helen and Shirley's support. I find it so rewarding to see them out of the sports context, because I see a lot more of their personalities as I am not just there as a coach. We have planned day trips to the seaside and the aquarium in Skegness. We also arranged a day out to a rhubarb farm so they could see and learn how food is grown and prepared.

At the end of each S.A.N.D. Season, we try to have a picnic before the summer holidays. In 2018 we decided to go to Thorsby Park and booked a private bird of prey demonstration. I love birds of prey and was really looking forward it. It was a lovely evening, and the hosts were amiable.

They were fantastic with the children, they got really close with all kinds of birds and got to hold them, Including owls and a great eagle. They just loved the experience! It was great seeing the kids overcome their fears and having the opportunity to hold such spectacular birds. The birds flew in between and all around them. I was ever so pleased when an owl decided to land directly on my head! I also got to hold a vast eagle. What a terrific encounter. I am not sure who enjoyed it more, the kids or me!

Archery

The S.A.N.D. club

2
FIRST RADIO INTERVIEW

In March 2013, I did my first ever live radio show. It was for a local community radio station in Clowne, which is the other side of Worksop.
I was invited by the presenter to talk more about my life and issues after reading my first book 'Life Rolls On.'

I saw this as an excellent opportunity to drive people to the website, advertise my first book and improve my confidence in speaking publicly.

In the van on the way there, I was very nervous.
I was going through some areas of questions I thought I would be asked as nothing had been rehearsed or pre-planned.
On the way there the road was very icy, which made me late. The show was meant to start at 8 pm, and I arrived 10 minutes before, so it was a little bit of a panic and a mad rush to get into the studio.

I was astonished by how small the actual studio was. It was only a tiny room full of computers, monitors and microphones. I knew it was just a small community radio, but I had expected the studio to be a significantly larger. I met the host and co-host, and they seemed friendly enough.

Initially, I was quite nervous but soon settled into the role. I introduced myself as Trev, which confused the presenter because the name on my book is Tony Trev Baker. I explained why, but she kept calling me Tony, even though I kept telling her I preferred to be called Trev. She must have done this about ten times and she really drove me insane.

I knew the first question I would be asked, was about the day of the injury, this was difficult to talk about on air, I have explained it so many times in the past, but only to individuals or small groups. I found the best way to approach the interview was to treat it as if it was just a normal conversation and not get caught up in the fact that it was being transmitted over the radio.

I did get some challenging questions and tried to be careful with my responses, although I did find out the morning after, that I had cursed in the first few minutes, which I put down to nerves.

That morning, I sent a text around and had posted on Facebook that I was going on the radio. I don't know exactly how many people listened in, but it was quite amusing when the hosts mentioned that people, I knew were popping up in the chat room. So it was quite nice being able to send them a shout out.

We had a chat off-air about my care situation and what it feels like to have people around constantly. We tried to recreate the conversation while on air, but it was quite awkward, as the carer with me at the time was working her notice period. I had to be aware of what I said, and it would've been preferable to not have her in studio, but with all the chaos she was invited in.

I was asked all sorts of questions, for example how I felt directly after my injury? How did I think in the first few months? How did I get through it? What was it like having to eat on my back? How did I feel about having care needs done by someone else? I was undoubtedly happier when I was able to talk about my involvement with Back Up, skiing and sailing.

In the last part of the interview, I was able to focus on the positives like going to college, getting involved in sports coaching, working with the S.A.N.D. (See Ability Not Disability) sports club, earning my degree and my new business venture. I found it particularly hard to talk about as I had initially contacted the company and asked their advice. Due to the fact, that the company doesn't advertise I wasn't able to mention them. I kept directing people to my website to find out more details, although the host kept pushing for more information, which I was unable to give.

I had a good chat with the host and co-host about offering both the services and the business opportunity off-the-air and they seemed interested. Ironically, I found out that she had joined as a partner under someone else and did well with it. You win some you lose some! I quite enjoyed the experience of going on the radio, it gave me more confidence in my speaking.

I was delighted, a couple of days later, when I found out my uncle had recorded the whole interview on his Dictaphone and sent it to me on a memory stick. It felt good listening back. I thought I presented myself well and gave a great insight psychologically, physically and emotionally into a life after spinal cord injury.

3
SAILING

I first heard about a project called Sailability a few years ago and knew that their purpose and aim was to cater for disabled people sailing. I went to visit one of the clubs on Rutland Water, but they didn't seem very helpful and I never actually got to go out on the water. I knew there were clubs with good reputations, near my dad's in Norfolk, but Norfolk is too far for a weekend hobby.

One of my friends told me about a club in Newark called Girton Sailing Club, he sails there quite often. He told me he had seen people in wheelchairs getting in and out of boats, so I decided to give them a call. It was near the end of the season, and the person in charge said that he wasn't going to be available for the last couple of sessions, but he said to come anyway and have a go.

As luck would have it, my dad who is a keen sailor was travelling back from Wales to Norfolk, and I arranged to meet him there.
Everyone was amicable, helpful and keen to get me out on the water.
I carefully drove my powerchair onto the jetty, and they used a hoist to get me onto the boat, although it

seemed that no one was able to figure out how to put the sling on properly and getting a buoyancy aid on was a nightmare, as they have no give in them at all.

The boats are purposely designed to be extraordinarily buoyant, so there is no chance of tipping over. It was a little 2-man dinghy with plenty of legroom, and with a bit of time and patience, it was quite easy to get me in.

The dinghy had a lever in the middle, which was attached to the rudder that I was able to grab hold of in order to steer the vessel. I had no solid grip, so it was hard to keep a hold on it.

The feeling of being on the water and away from the wheelchair was terrific. I felt a sense of liberation and exhilaration. When the sailboat picked up some wind and got some speed, it felt great.

I noticed my dad on the jetty, the instructor asked if he would like to join me in the boat. So, we headed back to fetch my dad. The instructor got out and my dad got in. It was a wonderful feeling. After all my we had been through over the years, to be out on the water together was an experience I will never forget, and I doubt he will. Nothing else mattered at that moment other than a father and son being together in a boat on a lovely sunny day.

I went back the next week, it was another sunny day. The last time I managed to get onto the jetty okay, but it was quite hard work, because the powerchair took a bit of pushing. This time I decided to go in my manual chair for safety reasons and to make it easier for everyone else. I never use my manual wheelchair unless I have to or if safety is involved.

There was a chap stood on the land near the jetty with a buoyancy aid on, wearing a cap and shades. I introduced myself, and he introduced himself. We both chatted happily for 10 to 15 minutes when he said, "by the way, I am completely blind." To which I replied, "by the way, I am in a wheelchair." There was a moment of reflection as it sank in that neither of us was aware that the other person had a disability, had I been in my powerchair he would have heard the motor, but the manual wheelchair was quiet.
It was such a beautiful moment where there was no preconceived idea of each other's disability, there were no judgments, no need to explain impairments. We were just two people who met and started talking straight away and wanted to enjoy the freedom of being on the water.

Winter seemed to drag, and I was looking forward to going sailing regularly and meeting more people with disabilities.

Water doesn't care about the person's condition, or ailments and sailing is a fantastic sport that should be enjoyed by all.

I managed to get out on the water a few times the first year I found sailing, but I always felt like a passenger. I was keen for a new year to start going back to Girton Sailing Club on Saturday mornings.

I have had some outstanding experiences on the water. It was a fantastic feeling and going sailing with my brother was also unique and enjoyable. I would have loved to sail with my friend Marcus who introduced me to the club (Marcus is a great friend and was climbing with me when I had my accident, and we were biking buddies.) We did get the chance of being on the water together, but he was in his boat. It still felt good though to be doing an activity together.

The lakes are situated in a beautiful area, and while being out on the water the Red Arrows have flown above us, I have also seen a Vulcan flying over the lake.

The people at the club have always been friendly and helpful, but there haven't always been enough volunteers to help get me out on the water. I really liked the club because they did bonfires and quiz nights. I found out about a more prominent club a further 30 minutes away.

When I first turned up there, it was evident that they were better geared up than Girton, with more volunteers and more boats. There also seemed to be a better atmosphere there, where people just sat around socialising.

The first time I went to this club, I was amazed by the size of the lake. Typically, there was no wind, but the club didn't seem bothered by this. They started preparing the sailboats with oars so people could still go out and have a row around the lake.

They told me they would take me out on the safety boat. It was good to be able to go around the lake a bit faster. As much as I like sailing, I'm quite partial to some speed, and feeling the wind in my face and feeling the power as it turned and moved around the water was great.

The second time I went to this particular club, it was a bit windier, and they started to prepare a two-person dinghy. I didn't mind going out in 2-man boats, but I was never actually in control, and I struggled with the actual rudder.

They asked me if I would like to go out on my own, which had always been a personal goal of mine, to be able to sail solo and independently. The volunteers prepared a different boat and hoisted me into it. The rudder was central in between my legs, and they set the sail at a certain tension.

At first, I was quite nervous about being in a boat on my own, but they said that the safety boat would follow me, and the nerves soon passed. Once I was on the water, I felt completely free. I never actually thought I would be able to be in a sailboat entirely on my own, but there I was doing it!

I was amazed at how well I could control it, and the wind conditions were just perfect to be able to get the hang of sailing, and how the craft felt.
I did manage to pick up speed a few times. It was exciting and liberating to achieve this goal. I was determined to sail back to the jetty without assistance and managed it correctly, which I was delighted about.

The club showed me some electronic server joysticks that they said I should be able to use so I could gain more independence and control. The boat was set up so that by moving the joystick left, and right it moved the rudder left and right, and when I pushed the joystick forward it let the sail out, and when I pulled the joystick back it tightened up the sail.

I found this method a lot easier to control and a lot more fun. I felt pleased and confident that I had reached my goal of being able to sail solo. I went out 2 or 3 times and was starting to gain some confidence.

I had mentioned that I felt I would be better if we adapted the seat, so it was more bucketed, which they did for me.

As soon as I started sailing and left the jetty, something didn't feel right, and I didn't have any control over it. The volunteers had set the sail far too tight, and it was just catching the wind. Initially, this was quite distressing, but I didn't see it as being a problem. Then the wind caught the sail fast and threw the boat to one side and that threw me to one side. I was unable to rectify my balance and started panicking. Then the wind caught the ship again while I was leaning over the side.

The sailboat didn't capsize, although I nearly fell overboard and was hanging out over the side with my face and my ear in the water. This was very scary, especially when you are physically unable to correct your balance or grab onto anything. I was terrified and wasn't sure if the boat would go over, I didn't think it would, but my main concern was falling out into the lake.

Luckily, I hadn't gone far from the jetty so was visible and I could hear panic on the walkie-talkies to get the safety boat to me as quickly as possible.
Thankfully the safety team was only a couple of minutes away, and they were able to make the sailing boat more stable.

The boats are designed not to capsize, but the club said it was the scariest thing they had seen in 6 years of running the Sailability project.

There was someone already at the jetty so I couldn't go straight in. My every instinct was telling me to get out and get back on dry land. While talking to the safety team though I realised it was near impossible for the boat to tip over, I also kept thinking to myself that if I did get out, I knew I wouldn't get back in. I had to dig into my inner strength and resilience to decide to stay in the boat.

When we got to the jetty, we put some padding under my elbows to help with my balance, and we reset the sail. I was glad that I did manage to stay in and continued sailing. I felt quite tense every time the wind caught the sail.

I stayed out for about 20 minutes and had a perfect time. I was delighted at how much control I did have and was able to sail back into the jetty correctly.

I was ever so relieved, although quite shaken up, and delighted to get back into my wheelchair and back on solid land.
The club members and volunteers said it looked hazardous and they thought I was going in the water. Thankfully the boat never capsized, and I overcame this fear so I was able to continue my love of sailing.

Sailing with my dad

Sailing solo

4
LIKE A FISH OUT OF WATER

At the start of 2013, I had problems with my powerchair. I knew the chair was getting old but kept sending it back for different repairs, batteries and a new controller. I had spent around £500 on repairs and was hoping that the chair would at least last for another year or so, or ideally until my business started to pay some money.

Unfortunately, this wasn't the case. I had arranged to go to a sports coaching session in it, but when we parked, the chair would not turn on at all. I was stuck in my van in a powerchair that didn't work. We tried to disconnect everything and clean everything, but it just wouldn't turn on.

The only option seemed to be, to take it back to Clarke and Partners, which was where it was purchased and see if they could get me out of the van and out of the chair. They managed to get the chair out of my vehicle but said it would cost more money to do a diagnostic test and guessed that it was probably the motors that had died.

I had had enough and decided it wasn't worth spending any more money on the chair. While I was in a foul mood and annoyed, I decided to look at new chairs. They didn't have a great selection, but they did have a lovely chair for £6500, so I arranged a demo, although I didn't fancy spending that kind of money.

I knew I had a busy week planned, so the idea of dragging out my manual chair, which is far too small for me, offers no back support and is extremely uncomfortable, was unbearable. The limited mobility in my arms means I cannot control it at all. It was a very frustrating couple of weeks and quite an eye-opener and a reminder of my disability.

I couldn't go and look at things as and when I wanted to. I had to direct my carers where to push me, which is incredibly frustrating, especially when you are not used to having someone behind you.
While being pushed in a wheelchair at a Paralympic Meet and Greet, and my carer stopped to talk to somebody. I found this to be incredibly frustrating because I had my back to them, and I couldn't turn around. My carers are very used to me just wandering around and doing my own thing that my carer just forgot. The Paralympian was initially shocked that I had just been left pointing in the wrong direction, but she did find it funny!

I did an inclusive wheelchair basketball coaching session while in the manual wheelchair. It was great that everyone else that was able-bodied had adapted wheelchairs to sit in for basketball, but it was more challenging to manoeuvre me around during the session. Trying to coach and deliver a course while trying to communicate where I needed to be was indeed a hindrance and I kept finding that the coach would call everyone into the middle and I would be left there like a spare part.

I also attended a business event and found it incredibly frustrating and annoying that I wasn't able to move around to talk to people, I just sat there and hoped people would come and talk to me.

Ironically it was probably the busiest couple of weeks I had planned. I managed to make it to every appointment and meeting. I even went to London to see the network headquarters for Utility Warehouse despite being in constant discomfort, pain and frustration.
Each time I had to get into the chair, I knew it was going to be hard work, but I didn't quit and kept on rolling!

I was ecstatic after a couple of weeks when I came across a few different chairs and found one which was suitable, comfy, smooth and easy to drive, as it could spin around in its own space. I was even more pleased by the fact that it retailed for £5500. I only paid £1400 for it, and it had 14 minutes of use. I'm not a fan of rear wheel drive powerchairs. Although they have power, they don't quite have the manoeuvrability of mid-wheel drive ones. The first chair that I had was by a company called Pride, and the new model that I bought was by the same manufacturer, but it was a new state-of-the-art machine. I chose this for a reason, as I managed to get about ten years out of the previous chair and I had indeed given it some hammer over the years, so I knew the chair could take my abuse. The chair proved its worth over and over again.

I often make plans to meet my dad and his partner in various places. He lives in Norfolk, and I don't get to see him that often, we arranged to meet at a National Trust stately home. I was running a bit early so decided to pop into McDonald's for a quick bite to eat. Here I found out that my chair wouldn't turn on which was an error that I had never seen before. We tried turning it on and off a few times, but it just wouldn't turn on. I checked the Internet for a solution but couldn't find anything. Luckily after a few attempts, it turned itself on.

It would've been a pain if I travelled about an hour and a half and ended up being stuck in the van and unable to see my folks. I found this started happening more and more regularly with the chair, so I took it back for maintenance, and it needed a new motor. I opted for a second hand one. After that, the chair seemed fine for a bit, but it kept pulling to the left especially when exiting the ramp on my van. I hoped it would last another year or so. It's quite difficult to know with these things at what point they just become worn out, and a new powerchair needs to be purchased. I am not your standard wheelchair user though, I do seem to put the chairs through their paces and take them places one probably shouldn't do, but that's what they are for.

One thing I have been very fortunate with over the years with my powerchairs is not having any punctures. I have been around the world by various means, using various chairs. I kept an emergency backup can of sealant in my rucksack to use for the tyres just in case I ever needed it.

The only time I ever had a puncture was when I went to a meeting and parked outside the hotel and travelled maybe 30 m. When I started moving the chair after the meeting, I knew straight away I had a puncture as the chair was going around in circles because it was a mid-wheel drive. Ironically, we could not access the valve with the canister I had. It was completely useless. I had to inch the chair and limp to the car park with someone pushing me. Once I got home, I called someone out to come and fix it that cost around £50. If it had happened anywhere else, it could have been disastrous. Thankfully I was just across from the car park!

After experiencing a puncture, and the hassle that went with it, my brother put some goo inside the tyres so that this would not happen again.

My second chair did very well, but things did go wrong with it, so I kept sending it for maintenance. Every time it was taken back for repairs, I knew I would be without it for a week or so. This was frustrating so I would apologise to my carers in advance for my language and crappy mood.

Once I burnt out another motor on a cruise ship halfway around the world. My chair overheated and kept veering left which was a challenge. We eventually realised the strain of getting on and off the ship caused this. So, we disengaged the motor and relied on brute strength to get on and off. I was determined not to let it ruin my cruise! I did spend a fair bit of time phoning mobility shops around the

Canaries to try to purchase a manual wheelchair. Thankfully my chair made it to the last port before it perished in Portugal. We were about 15 minutes from the ship which meant it was a fair trek for those that had to push me back.

Luckily, we only had two days left at sea before we were due back home. It was back-breaking work for my carer who had to push me around in a powerchair that weighed 250 kg and kept veering more and more to the left.

I had already repaired this chair, but it did not feel right. I used it for about five years, and I did not want to spend any more money on it. I referred back to where I had bought the chair and remembered what a deal I got. As soon as I got home, I found their site on eBay, and as luck would have it, they had the latest state-of-the-art model in stock. I phoned them straight away to arrange a viewing. The new chair was in great condition, without a scratch! It retailed at £6500, but they had it on offer for £1400 but accepted £1300. The seat needed adjusting, so I arranged to pick it up a few days later. There are other manufacturers that make mid-wheel drive chairs, but I preferred to stick to the brand I know well, Pride. All my powerchairs were from Pride.

It's one thing buying a new chair but fitting in one is another story. I am 6 foot 4, so a few adjustments had to be made, such as, lowering the footplate, tilting back the backrest and adjusting the position of the controller so I could reach it. I have always used a gel cushion that helps to alleviate some pressure, but I had been struggling with it, so I decided to look for a semi-inflatable cushion called a Roho. They are very expensive. I found a generic version in Taiwan for £80. One of my carers asked how I was getting on with the new chair, and I explained about the cushion. Unexpectedly she happened to have an original £500 one at home that her cat was sleeping on! She said I could have it! It was very comfy.

Once I had fitted out the chair so I could drive it better, I took it for a couple of runs. It was incredibly smooth because of the suspension. The motor was ever so quiet, and one could feel the gears changing gear when going uphill or on rough terrain. I was delighted with the outcome and hoped it would last a few years.

I did make a stupid mistake though. We tried putting some of the goo inside the new tyres to avoid punctures, thinking that prevention is better than cure, but somehow, we ended up losing the valve. This meant I had to call the repairman again to put in a new inner tube, which was a waste of £50.

One thing that does amaze me about these chairs is the fact that they do not come with lights! I am disabled, not a vampire. 5 or 6 thousand-pound chairs, yet no lights. There have been a number of times I have felt unsafe and invisible while crossing car parks or roads. My brother added some lights to my chair for my 40th birthday. It made such difference, I was able to see bumps, cracks and the pavement edges.

The knowledge that my chair is visible from behind really gave me peace of mind. Unfortunately, a front light cracked while getting the batteries out of my old chair, so I found different ones on eBay that were much better and brighter. Thankfully we were able to add a toggle switch that I could operate myself to turn the lights on and off.

I have been very fortunate that my dad had put money away for me to buy different disability equipment, although the long-term plan was to be able to afford things myself.

Just like able-bodied people take their bodies for granted, I take my powerchair for granted, and without it, I am like a fish out of water.

5
RANDOM STUFF

Life can have a firm desire to survive. While we were
redoing my pond and building a larger surface area for
water, we placed my fish in a large barrel. We put a
makeshift lid on the barrel as it was only for a couple
of days. One evening while I was sat on my own
pondering the complexities of life, (I had just been to
a friend's dad's funeral), my cat appeared through the
cat flap with a lovely fish in its mouth. I shouted at the
cat, and it placed the fish in the middle of the living
room floor. My carer arrived at 10, and the poor fish
had been on the floor for about an hour and a half. I
told him about the dead fish in the living room, but
believe it or not, it was not dead! When he picked it
up, it started flapping so he threw it back in the water
and it swam off. I have a feeling it must have jumped
out of the barrel and my cat brought it in as if to say,
"Dad, I think this belongs in the water." So, I decided
to call the fish Lucky.

A carer and I went to the cinema to watch
Independence Day, it was raining heavily outside.
While watching the film, I felt a drop of water on my
head. I thought it was just a drop, but it continued, and
I ended up pretty wet. I was at the back, so I knew it

wasn't kids messing around. I repositioned my chair and enjoyed the rest of the film.

The rain had dripped through the roof and short-circuited the lift, so when we came out the elevator wasn't working. We were on the top floor, so we were offered a free film to watch by the cinema staff that was to start in 15 minutes. This was perfect timing and such a treat. They were very apologetic and we were given free food and drink; we were pleased with that. By the end of the second film, the lift was fixed. I was sent down with an engineer just in case. The manager was ever so apologetic that he gave us six free cinema tickets. What a great gift especially as when I go to the cinema my carers get in free, and we usually split the difference. We got to watch six free films, 2 of which were in the Imax.

When I had just started studying sport, my tutor booked me on a training course at Sheffield University that was about making all sport more accessible for disabled people. We arrived at the venue to find that there was no wheelchair access. The sports hall was up some steps, I had to go all the way around the building to get into the room. The organisers were very embarrassed about this and said they weren't expecting somebody in a wheelchair, which ironically was what the course was about. Having access for all. I think they learnt a valuable lesson that day–when planning a sports session, you never know who is going to turn up. Make sure that the venues are accessible.

One of the strangest appointments I had from U.W. (Utility Warehouse) was an elderly lady, I call Mad Maurine. She was a lovely lady, but completely mad and very religious. There was a significant step to the kitchen, and there was no way I could get my ramp up onto it. However, she was convinced that Jesus had sent her to me for a reason, and she was confident that if I wanted it hard enough, I would be able to get up the step and get out the chair. I kept pointing out to her that I was paralysed and wheelchair-bound. She went on for about 5 minutes, she was convinced I would be able to will myself up the steps. Not surprisingly the appointment didn't get much better after that. She was barking mad and suffice to say she didn't close the deal.

The new term had just started, and I was talking to a parent of one of our children at the S.A.N.D. club. Her daughter is a very headstrong, lovely girl that has a disability and uses a wheelchair. We always try to adapt things around her that she might find difficult. The parent was saying that the new head of her special needs school wouldn't let this child play Boccia. The parent even offered to take her daughter in her vehicle. The reason the head had come to this conclusion was because Boccia wasn't suitable for a child in a wheelchair! Boccia is a game designed for people with disabilities and people who use wheelchairs, even one of the rules states that everyone must remain seated.

Not only is she very good at the game and enjoys playing it but also, it's one of the only games she can participate in as part of a team, so to have it taken away by a so-called head of a special needs school is beyond a joke! The whole point is inclusion. The entire situation upset the child, and the parent. That school should know better!

Boccia is a fantastic game, players of all ages enjoy it. One of our volunteers at the S.A.N.D. club goes above and beyond the call of duty. She works at a primary school and she has tons of kids wanting to play, they love playing the game, yet the school will not buy a proper Boccia set, which admittedly is expensive. She has to do training sessions in the corridors on her dinner break using rubbish balls. She goes out of her way to accommodate the children and take them to all the local competitions, and most of the time the teams win! The school will not provide adequate equipment or allocate a dedicated time slot to play on a smooth floor to give the children a chance to practice. It's sad that the school does not recognise how important the game is. A lot of the children who don't want to play mainstream sports are being let down.

I wanted to go out and see some fireworks, so I did a Google search for the Retford Bonfire Night 2017 and found out that there was a display about half a mile away at a local football ground. It sounded like it was a good event with small rides, live music with a bar and food. When we arrived at the football ground, we could see some fireworks going off. I thought this was a kid's display. The car park was empty, so when another car pulled up next to us, we asked if there was another entrance and where the fireworks were. She said she was there for a friend's party, I looked back on my phone, and it turned out the event was back in 2007, so I was ten years too late! Suffice to say I felt a bit of a pillock!

I have a wet room, which has caused me a lot of damp problems over the years. It has brought in slugs which is not only disgusting but has also made my cats sick! The wet room kept overflowing and not draining all the water out properly, so we called in some contractors. They couldn't do anything about the slugs, but one of the contractors said that the reason it wasn't emptying properly was because of the type of shower gel I was using. What a load of nonsense!

When they came for another evaluation a few years later, all the skirting boards were rotten. Apparently, there were holes in the piping so every time we used the shower, water was going everywhere. Eventually, the job was correctly finished, and I had a new wet room fitted, which took months to do that was a bit of a nightmare!

I enjoy playing online role-playing games such as Lord of the Rings and Star Wars. I am restricted to what I can play on the computer, because of the type of mouse I use as I cannot use game consoles. I can control everything on screen apart from the jump button that is activated by the space bar, so every now and then I have to ask a carer to press it to jump the unusual step. I play the games to pass the time and escape reality but even in a Galaxy Far Far Away or being lost in Middle Earth, my virtual characters are still hindered by steps, society and the environment, just like I am in the real world.

When I am at home, I don't sit in my wheelchair. I sit in an adapted chair. I feel more relaxed and I am more comfortable when I am in a standard chair. People see me as normal when they can't see the wheelchair. About ten years ago, if not more. I bought a chair off eBay for around £150. We put some door handles on the back so it could be pulled, and we drilled in some wooden struts along the base and finally we put some large castor wheels on so we could move the chair. Eventually, the back weakened, and didn't offer any support. I spoke to my Occupational Therapist about the possibility of getting a new one, because I had never claimed one before, he reckoned it shouldn't be a problem.

An assessor was sent to evaluate the chair and agreed that my makeshift chair wasn't offering much support and that I could get a brand-new one that retailed about £4500.

When the sales rep arrived, he said he had heard about my makeshift chair off eBay and that he was looking forward to seeing it. When you're living life on a tight purse string, you have to learn to adapt and make the most of things. He told me he had never seen anything quite like it. He was highly amused, and I was amazed that the chair had lasted so long.

I got a fantastic brand-new chair. It is incredibly comfortable, very supportive, it is effortless to manoeuvre and it has various settings for reclining. I have no idea how they can justify the cost of it though. I wouldn't even have considered spending this kind of money at the start of my journey especially when you compare it to having a vehicle or a powerchair.

One incident made me laugh, due to the fact that I can't handle physical money or my wallet so normally my carers will go to the bar for me. On one occasion while buying me a pint, my carer was refused service without his ID, even though he was in his late 30s. He explained to the bar lady that he was buying the pint for his disabled boss. He came back laughing and was very pleased he had been refused a pint because he did not have any ID. So, I went to the bar with my carer, and I asked for a pint, which she started to pour. When she asked for the money my carer had to give it to her. She was quite confused because she had just turned him away and would just not give him the pint. I had to explain that the pint was for me, and I couldn't physically handle money or pick up the pint. She eventually gave up in the end and gave us the pint. It was funny seeing her moral dilemma.

One of my favourite places to visit is the Yorkshire Wildlife Park. It's about 25 minutes away from where I live. I love animals and hate seeing them in cages. It is a massive park and easily accessible. Each habitat is enormous and caters to the animal's needs and environment.
I have been going there for a few years now and have seen the park continuously develop and grow.
They have tigers, lions, a leopard, rhinos, giraffe, zebra, bears and even polar bears and so much more.

You can tell that the animals are well looked after and are very happy in their environments. The park has established itself as a place for conservation and rehomed animals from around the world.

I find the place very therapeutic so whenever I'm feeling low or fed up, I go there. It's a great place to meet family and people and have a good wander around for the day.

The park always plans exciting events such as, Christmas fairs, Halloween events; music in the summer and even showed the World Cup.

I have an overhead tracking hoist in my bedroom. When I first moved into my home, the council put in a unit that lasted for years but eventually needed replacing. It kept breaking down and then ultimately was unrepairable. The whole lift was replaced with a second-hand one, which has never been right from day one. It is continually being checked and monitored, but it is mostly unresponsive.

For a couple of months recently, it wasn't working very well and would struggle a bit to go up and down. I called an engineer in who agreed that the controller needed replacing so he ordered one through his company. It took nearly two weeks for someone to come out and replace the controller. I went to bed that night, and it still did not go up correctly, so I phoned the council and explained the lift wasn't working right.

The initial engineer came by and noticed straightaway that the company had replaced the controller with a second-hand one, which he had seen lying around the warehouse. A couple of days later I had to call the engineer back again. The lift still did not feel right! This time a different engineer arrived, and was adamant there was nothing wrong with it. We could see how hard he was pressing the button, eventually it stopped responding. It also slipped, which it had never done before. It was evident that the whole unit was broken. It took over a month and numerous calls and engineer visits to get a new one. Surely it should have been a priority to make sure I was safe! Ironically after countless visits, I received a letter from the council saying the lift needed servicing. The lack of communication and urgency was a joke. Without a reliable, safe lift I would potentially be stuck in bed!

Christmas is always quite odd! Due to the fact I have different carers I have to try and be sneaky and remember what I bought for different people. If I'm expecting something through the post, I have to be careful who opens it. I often have to get one person to wrap one lot of the presents and somebody else to wrap the other lot, to at least keep the element of surprise. I am physically unable to unwrap presents myself. We usually find the best way to do this is for somebody to loosen off all the Sellotape, I can then slide my finger in and try and rip some of the paper off. Which never works, although I can often see a little bit of present, then I have to get someone to help take off the rest of the wrapping paper. One way or another we always find a way of adapting to the situation.

6
PHYSIOTHERAPY

When I first had my injury the most important thing
was physiotherapy. It was essential to try and get as
much movement and strength back as possible. Over
the years I haven't done much physiotherapy, I do
have an exercise machine, which is like an automatic
bike that stretches my legs and my arms, but I don't
use it much. It's like a torture device and feels
uncomfortable to use, and it takes a long time for my
body to recover. I contacted local authorities to see if I
would be able to get any physiotherapy, as the
stiffness and tightness have gotten worse over the
years.

A lady came out to see me and did an assessment.
One of the first things she was critical about was the
fact that I have two pillows under my head. She
questioned why I had this and how long I had used
them for. I replied, "I'm over 40 years old and it is my
decision how many pillows I want or need, and I
know what is comfortable for me". I realized that we
were probably not going to get along, as we didn't see
eye to eye!

I planned to use a trained expert to loosen up my
joints and muscles and then to be able to show my

carers some basic stretches. The physiotherapist was pathetic. She could barely move my legs, which was the whole point of having physiotherapy, and she had no techniques or skills to loosen me up. All she kept saying was "your legs are too stiff, and I can't move them" in a pathetic voice. I knew my legs were stiff which was why I was getting physiotherapy–to get my circulation going and relieve some spasm. My legs were not that bad as my carers could get trousers on and roll me every day!

I found this quite disheartening and demotivating, I only saw her a couple of times and didn't get into a routine. A friend of mine recommended a physiotherapist to me. I arranged an assessment, but I don't think he had come across someone who had suffered a spinal injury. The body reacts very differently after such trauma. We spent a lot of time talking, and he did some soft tissue work on my arms, but not that much passive movement. I felt a bit better after it, but I didn't think he had the skills to work with me and there was no way I could afford private treatment.

A few years later, I was struggling within myself (see The Negative Chapter). I was speaking to a lady about personal finances for my care, and she asked if I received regular physiotherapy. I told her that I did not. The reason she asked was that she could see by my terrible posture and that my shoulders and back were slumping forward, which was what was causing my pain and discomfort. She said I should be able to get some funding for regular physiotherapy. I felt it would benefit me, as I didn't want to get any worse.

As luck would have it, I was going out that day, and we called into a nearby gym. They recommended a lady to me who was experienced in working with disabled people. This was fantastic as it was going to save me time searching the Internet for the right physiotherapist.

I spoke to this lady on the phone, and I could tell we would get along, and that she was knowledgeable, so I arranged an assessment with her. She was very hands-on straightaway. I contacted the social worker that asked for a written evaluation from me and the physiotherapist and how physiotherapy would help me. I managed to get funding straight away for six months of physiotherapy. This made a massive difference in my life and helped things like dressing and rolling and helped me get more comfortable.

I was amazed at how quickly I was able to get funding and start receiving some treatment. Typically, it can take forever to get any funding, but I started therapy before receiving any money. I had confirmation emails, and the physiotherapist was quite happy with this.

She started with her initial assessment, and I could tell she was very knowledgeable, and we would get on. She had lots of experience with spinal injury, strokes and neurological conditions.

She was very good at explaining each treatment she used and how it would affect my body long-term and short-term. She was also very good and very patient at showing my carers what movements they should do regularly.

Sometimes we had a full stretch on the bed, and she would do one side of my body and show the carers what to do on the other side, we were also doing stretches in my chair and explaining how to get the best possible movement. I found this great as it saved the hassle of getting out the chair and what stretches to do while sitting.

We did some exercises on my back where I was in the sling, attached to the overhead hoist on the edge of the bed, and she rotated my back. These were movements I hadn't been able to do since my injury. It does take my body a long time to recover. When I am out and about and feeling stiff, it's great knowing that my carers are trained and feel confident and comfortable enough to give me a stretch to make things like driving my chair easier and safer.

Funding did eventually come to an end, but the aim was to train my carers enough so that a routine of physiotherapy and exercise could be maintained. We were able to achieve this from the fantastic training and continued to do physiotherapy.

7
BACK UP MENTORING

A couple of years after I had got my degree and wrote my first book, I came across a post on Facebook from the Back Up Trust looking for Mentors. They were looking for people who had suffered a spinal injury to help other people early on in their injury with various issues and help them get a better understanding of what they were going through with guidance and support.

Back Up was a significant factor in helping me to gain independence and getting my life back in the early days of my spinal injury. They gave me my confidence back and gave me an awareness of what I could do and achieve. They also gave me something, which I had not felt for a long time, Hope!

With Back Up, I have skied, sailed and done a wide range of outdoor pursuits including quad biking. I have even been into hospitals and told people who were newly injured about my experiences with Back Up.

In the early days of my injury, I could have done with someone who had been through everything years down the line to help with one-on-one guidance, advice and motivation.

I, therefore, felt this would be a great direction for me to pursue. I thought I would be able to help people going through similar situations, as I have been through it myself and participated in all the activities. I earned myself a degree in counselling, I am now a qualified sports coach, and I have also written a book about my life, injury and recovery.

They arranged to do an interview with me over the phone. We spent about 45 minutes going through what it would entail and what I could offer. The role wasn't going to be a paid position, it was purely voluntary, and I was more than willing to give my time to help others.

I detailed everything I had been through and explained what I had done over the past 17 years. A couple of weeks later I got a phone call from them. I was excited thinking how this would be a positive step for me.

However, they turned me down! I asked them why they had turned me down to be a mentor, and I had answered a question regarding what I would do or say to a child that had been bullied at school incorrectly.

I do not remember what I had said, but I was coming from a person-centered train of thought. I would have worked with the individuals in a safe environment and explored how they were feeling, what they were going through and helped them find the skills to cope and find their inner strength to accept responsibility and rise above it, or something along those lines. I don't remember.

I was amazed that they turned me down just because of the way I chose to answer a verbal question with no preparation. If there are people more capable than me, then that's fine.
It hit me hard being turned down for this position. Not being able to offer my experiences to help someone else was very disappointing as I felt I could have made a difference and had a massive impact on someone else's life and recovery.

What more experience would I have needed to be able to mentor a newly spinal injured person? Other than having been through it all myself, living independently with carers, excellent communication skills, a positive mental attitude, written a book about the very subject and even a professional qualification saying that I can cope with any condition and living with a spinal injury myself.

Never mind all the activities and travelling and methods of adaptation I have encountered over the years. I want to meet this person who has done more than me, to give me some pointers!

I could have pursued this further down the line. However, the timing was not right for me because other priorities required my time and focus.

8
THE BEST £10 I SPENT

My carers asked me what I would like for my 30th birthday, and I replied: "I would love a kitten." We never really had pets growing up due to my brother's allergies. I remember we had a couple of lizards in a tank and a couple of budgies but nothing to call my own.

When I moved into town before my injury, the environment wasn't right for a pet. But after I had been living at my home after my injury for a few years, I felt it would be great to have a kitten of my own.

My carers chipped in together and bought me a kitten. I'll always remember when I was introduced to 2 kittens. They came from a pet rescue place, and they showed me, two sisters. Their names were Sasha and Tasha, and they were only nine weeks old. They were tiny, and they said that if I wanted a soft lap cat, then Sasha would be the one. I agreed that Sasha seemed to be a lovely, friendly cat, but the ladies didn't want to separate the two because they were sisters.

Having never owned a cat before and with my disability but knowing that the responsibility of looking after them would rely on the carers so, I thought that two would be too much hassle. However, they offered me Tasha for £10 including vaccinations, so I accepted this, and she became the best £10 I've ever spent!

The day was the afternoon of my birthday, and I remember accepting them both and then going out to the pub to meet some mates. I was only down the road so one of the carers, Dawn arranged to pick me up.

Dawn was also the person who had sorted the kitten idea out in the first place. She didn't know they were coming that day and it was a lovely surprise for her. She saw one of the kittens and was pleased. She then saw the other one but thought it was the same one she had just seen. I didn't tell her I had 2, they were both black and white and looked similar. You can imagine her surprise when she saw them both together!

Fourteen years on and they have been lovely, loyal pets. They are so loving, therapeutic, mischievous and playful. It's great whenever I go out or wake up in the morning, and they are there demanding attention.

They became very popular with my carers, which was excellent as there is only so much fuss and attention, I can physically give them. I can't physically drag them around. The good thing is that they are independent and when I go away on holiday, they are okay, as long as someone comes in and feeds them,

I once interviewed a new carer, and I had my social worker and team leader with me. One of the first things that came out of his mouth was that the cats would have to go outside, I replied "thanks for your time, but you're wasting your time if you don't like the cats." or something along those lines. Poor bloke didn't even take his coat off, he looked at me and said, "Is that it, interview over?" and I said, "pretty much." The look on his face was priceless, as was the social worker's.

I do find it frustrating not being able to feel how soft they are in my hands, as I have no sensation in my hands. I found this took a long time to accept, but I soon realised that just because I can't feel the fur, they can feel the love and attention and they don't care or judge. I do stroke them with my chin and forehead and they love that.

Tasha was fortunate when she was little. She came in one day and seemed fine, but I could see something on her face, so I had a closer look. She had been shot with a pellet gun, just under her eye and next to her nose was a lead pellet in her face. We took her to the vet, and it was safely removed with no harm done. Had it been millimeters, either way, she could have been blinded or lost her sense of smell.

Sasha really snuggles into my lap, and I can fuss and stroke her with my left arm and hand and still use my phone on my leg with my right hand. Tasha wasn't very affectionate to other people for a few years. She was my cat, and she always used to need to be near me whether it was on my lap or on the back of the chair or just nearby. Over the years Tasha became much needier and loved fuss from everyone. She was stubborn at times and often laid on my hands when I was trying to do something, I was always asking people to pick her up and move her. It's quite strange not being able to pick them up myself, but the cats knew this and played on it and got their way.

I'm often asked what the one thing is that made me change and accept my condition. There have been lots of various factors as discussed in this book and the previous, but the minute those cats appeared in my life, I felt like a new person. I had something to look after; something to fuss and love and something that gave me unconditional love back without any judgement.

It's true when they say cats have nine lives, they have both given us some scares. Sasha had to have some teeth removed, but she was never the same after. She always seems in discomfort during and after eating, so needs pain medication and toothpaste. She started looking scruffy and not cleaning herself and she got really matted up and was always dribbling, she wasn't very social either and she was not eating much. One of my carers shaved off lots of her fur and clumps, and a few weeks later she was back to her old self.

I went out one night and got home at about midnight to find my carer holding Tasha, she looked distraught. She said she had come on shift and Tasha had peed and pooed herself, which was unusual, and she was limp. We thought she had had a stroke as she could barely stand or hold her head up. She slept on me that night. I thought she was not going to wake up. In the morning she was unresponsive. Sasha came in and looked at Tasha wearily, Tasha lifted her paw about a centimeter and touched her sister. I thought that was going to be the last memory. We took her to the vet, thinking that was it, but she meowed a bit in the cage and showed a bit of spirit. The vet found a lump in her abdomen and gave her some steroids; thankfully she came home and picked up after a couple of days.

We kept giving her steroids for about three weeks, but unfortunately, she never got any better. I took her to the vet, but the lump had become more significant, and she wasn't eating or drinking much. The vet said there was nothing they could do. I could see she was struggling to hang on, she was such a fighter. I kept thanking her for being such a loyal friend, and to let it go.

I got up early one morning for a video training workshop I had paid for and looked at her and knew she did not have long, so I stayed at home with her. She knew I was there for her. We managed to catch a photo of her with a rainbow spectrum across her body from one of my ornaments. My carer said it was the rainbow bridge getting ready for her. She died the next day. I was so glad I listened to my instincts and did not leave her alone.

I had to make the tough decision to have her put to sleep, and the vet said they would come to my home. She passed away naturally at home, which was the best outcome I could have asked for. She left a massive hole in my heart and my carers, as many loved her.

Tasha always was the mischievous, dominant one, and she ruled the roost, especially when it came to food.

She would often swipe at Sasha, who had to wait to see what was left. Sasha seemed a bit lost for a couple of weeks afterwards. She soon accepted it though and realised she could eat as and when she wanted, demand attention and sit on my lap instead of having to fight for it.

It was a reminder that life is short and to cherish the small moments. During those three weeks I got some lovely photos and memories.

Sasha and Tasha (Tasha on the arm.)

9
THE BIG 4 ZERO

When I hit 40, I decided that I would throw a party. 40 is a significant milestone for anyone, but especially after having my injury 15 years previously, it felt like an even bigger milestone to me. I looked into where I could have it, but for me, there was only one real option.

When I was growing up, we always had parties at a social club called the B.R.S.A. Where we got up to all kinds of mischief while at school, during the sixth form and from 18 and onwards. I also celebrated my 21st there, so it felt like an appropriate venue.

The price to hire the venue was quite reasonable, and I decided on a fancy-dress theme. Wayne said he was quite happy to do an acoustic set and sing with his guitar and an old friend of mine called Cookie said he would play on the decks and do a mixture of modern music, dance and hip-hop.

I thought the best way of sorting out food was to ask people if they could bring a few sandwiches, sausage rolls, cake or anything they wanted. No one had a problem with this whatsoever. Everybody brought bits and bobs, and we ended up with far too much food.

The owner of the venue was a bit funny about putting things on the wall, which was fine, so we just put up a few balloons. However, I was very annoyed on the evening, over the use of the P.A. system. I had arranged to provide my own music, which was an acoustic singer with guitar, and the owner agreed to let us use their P.A. system. On the night, the owner threw a tantrum when we tried to set up our equipment. This would have been a nightmare and spoilt the evening if I would not have been allowed to have live music or music playing from the decks.

I definitely would not have paid, and I would have kicked up a storm. Luckily, we were able to use Wayne's P.A. system. In hindsight, I should have asked for a discount as I was quite appalled by how badly I was treated. I had hired a venue for a party, and I was told I had to use my own P.A. system, the reason I booked the room in the first place was for the sound system and a dance floor.

The owner was quite funny all night, and he did get himself into trouble, about halfway through the night when he came up to me and said there was a dubious bloke sitting on his own at the other bar. I investigated, and it turned out to be one of my carer's husbands. He had gone for a quiet pint and a bit of peace.

The night was a great success, and most people dressed up. I decided to recreate Peter Kay's Brian Potter from Phoenix Nights who is a grumpy old man in a wheelchair. I thought this would be appropriate especially as my party was in a working men's club. I didn't quite look like Brian Potter. It was more of a representation of what I'd be like as an old man, with an awful cardigan, shirt and tie, grey hair and a bald head, glasses and a grey moustache. I was pleased with the result. I think it looked pretty funny. There were some great costumes ranging from cowboys, a cyborg, wolves, Fred Flintstone, a black ghostbuster, just to name a few.

I was delighted with the number of friends who turned up from all walks of life.

Both sides of my family turned up, which was great! This was something that hadn't happened in a long time and the night was a complete success. It was excellent to catch up with people and celebrate. We had to tidy everything up at the end of the night and leave the place as we found it. We ended up with far too much food, and people had to take some home with them.

I seem to remember a lot of people piling into my van that probably wasn't safe as we were well overloaded and my carer drove a few people home. It was great fun and a grand celebration!

Great friends and a great celebration

10
FANCY DRESS

Fancy dress is quite a hard thing to do when you are a wheelchair user. The chair is such a massive thing, and it is tough to hide it and make a character that utilises the chair. For my 40th I had already used my Brian Potter idea up.

For my cousins 40th birthday, I came across a Stig costume that I thought was pretty funny. It was the classic white race suit and a helmet made out of material. I had to cut a section off the bottom so I could use a straw, which was a pain, but adaptation is the key to living with a disability. People were asking if I was the Stig in a wheelchair or I was the Stig. Either way, I just thought it was great being a racing driver in a powerchair.

For a mates Halloween fancy dress party, again this proved quite a tricky thing to solve. There are only really a few iconic people in wheelchairs in the movies, and most tend to use manual wheelchairs. Brian Potter, Lou and Andy from Little Britain, Ironside and then of course Charles Xavier from X-men who uses a powerchair with his mind. I didn't fancy shaving my head in October knowing we would be sitting outside. I may do this at some point and make my chair look like his futuristic one.

I opted for Lou and Andy from Little Britain, and my carer agreed to go as Lou. It was too obvious to go with Lou and Andy, as it was a Halloween theme. I decided to go as Andy making his impression of Freddy Krueger. I found a cheap clawed hand on ebay and got some latex that we put on my face and painted it red and yellow to give a burnt effect. I thought Andy would go to as little effort as possible to look like Freddy Krueger, so we got a red jumper and used gaffer tape to crudely make some black stripes across the jumper, making Freddy Krueger's iconic red and black striped jumper. I also had Andy's wig and glasses on. This confused people and that was my intention, it was clear that it was meant to be Freddy Krueger although Freddy Krueger doesn't wear glasses or have a bald head with long hair!

People started talking to me, and I would reply with Andy's catchphrases, such as, someone would say, "You don't look like Freddy Krueger there's something not right". And I would reply "yeah I know" or "I don't like it", then Wayne said, "Andy you wanted to come as Freddy Krueger, you say he's the epitome of a horrible monster, but you always wet yourself after watching his films"

It was funny when people realised it was two characters in one and it was Andy's version of Freddy Krueger.

Fancy dress is one thing and is fun and can be silly. I found myself going to more and more Comic Cons and was amazed at how much effort people went to, so they would look like their favourite superheroes, villains, and characters from games etc. This is known as Cosplay.

We went to another one and Wayne dressed up as Marty McFly from Back to the Future, which looked cool! I felt left out and asked him if he still had the cyborg mask, he wore for my 40th, which he had. The costume was a full latex cyborg head with a robotic eye that, when used with a downloadable app on a smartphone, the robotic eye moved around, in and out of the helmet and zoomed in and out as though it was scanning the target. When he used it with a leather jacket and rifle, he looked like the Terminator.

I said it would be a good idea if I were to get the mask and somehow utilise my chair and make it into a tank of some description to help make it into a feature!

We weren't sure at all how this would happen but figured there must be a way of attaching some plywood to the front, back and side of the chair. I started collecting gears and cogs, to make it look authentic. I mentioned the idea to my brother, and he came up with a couple of drawings that did look very effective. I really had no idea how we were going to pull it off, but where there's a will there's a way!

We stuck lots of paper together and made a rough template. I started looking for decals and stickers on eBay and found all sorts of things like electrical warning stickers, nuclear stickers, bullet holes and flames.

Kev (my brother) said he was talking to Jeff an architect, who is a good mate of mine, and specialises in building, roofing timber and does a lot of woodwork. They came up one day with all the equipment and tools and got to work. Kev had made a large Gatling style machine gun out of pipes to add to the effect.

The initial problem was getting in and out of the van, so we had to make something which could be adapted and added to the chair once we had got to the venue. On the chair itself, there are loops that we used to attach the chair into the van; they cut out the frames around the wheels and made brackets so that the side panels could just be clicked quickly into place. They did a fantastic job. They sat on the side of the chair perfectly and lifted on and off.

I felt it would be good to have a tank with a battering ram at the front of the chair so we came up with a wedge that would sit under my feet at the front of the chair. They did a great job between them and created two side panels, a panel for the back, the battering ram, a machine gun and brackets on the sides that held drainpipes, and various sized pipes that we made into missiles.

We sprayed the back and the sides black and started putting stickers on the panels and making missiles and nuclear canisters. I decided to spray the front ram silver, so it looked metallic. I had some black and yellow hazard tape that we put along the bottom so that it was visible, and people would be able to see and not trip over it. It looked pretty menacing. I came across some red flashing L.E.D. lights that we added just above the warning tape. I was delighted when I came across a black sticker that was like robot skull and crossbones wearing a gas mask. They looked perfect on the battering ram.

Everyone chipped in and did their bit of work. We smashed up a skybox and got some great circuitry, we drilled more holes in the back and made it look like the back of a tank. It seemed impressive, mean, aggressive and effective. We made missiles and rockets from bits of drainpipe and formed a cone at the end of each one and then decorated them with nuclear warning signs.

The first time I used it as a full setup, I was dressed in burnt military gear complete with dog tags, cyborg head, and knives attached to me for close up combat. We parked the car and started getting out all the bits, this chap was watching us with utter bewilderment and watched us put it all together. It was the first time we had seen it complete, and it looked fantastic. The chap asked us to wait 5 minutes, and he ran into the house to call his kids to come have a look. At this point, I knew we had created something special.

The reactions I got were much better than anticipated. People were just amazed at the level of creativity. You could see the look of shock on people's faces at seeing a cyborg driving a tank around with flashing lights and armed up to the helms. People were asking for photographs, and some kids were scared of it.

It looked effective against the backdrop of all the other settings and outfits. It was a bit of a nightmare to drive as I could only see out of 1 eye and had a big machine gun on the side and a 3-foot battering ram on the front.

I have used it four times, and each time I got the same response. The timing was great too as it was initially shown on the eve of Halloween and at the S.A.N.D. club the night after, so I prepared the tank again and went into the sports hall and just sat there in complete darkness with all my lights flashing. Luckily enough, a group of kids and staff all piled in at the same time and got a bit of a shock to see this tank driven by a cyborg sitting in the darkness.

I even won first prize in one of the costume parades. It's a great feeling having people looking at me in the wheelchair for a good reason and to get a response instead of people looking at me just because I'm in a wheelchair!

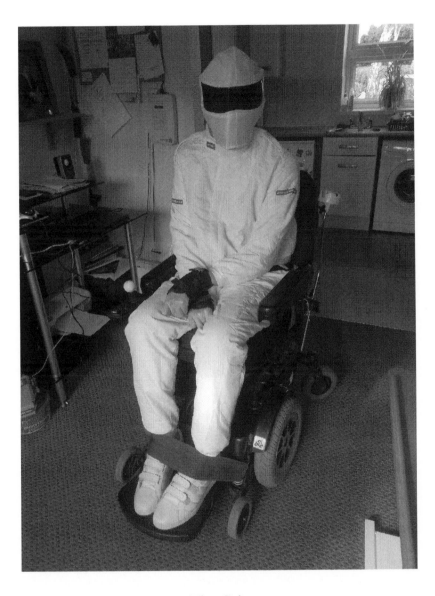

The Stig

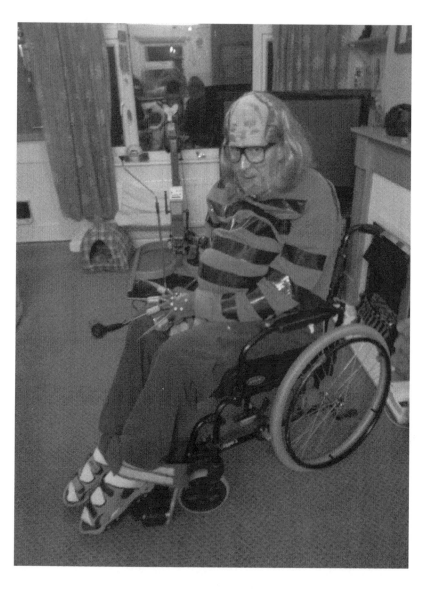

Andy as Freddie Krueger

Cyborg

11
POWERCHAIR FOOTBALL

I'm always looking for something different to do, and I was asked if I would like to try powerchair football. I'm usually on the side or coaching when it comes to sport, so I thought I'd give this a go.

The first time I went, I was hoisted into the chair, and the chair was set on speed 3. It was a little bit twitchy at first, and the joystick was placed quite a bit ahead of me and not in the right position. One of the coaches had already said that it couldn't be moved back, so I struggled straightaway by moving myself forward. I couldn't quite reach the joystick, so I went and spoke to him, and he was able to slide the armrest back a couple of inches, so the golf ball was in a better position.

I did get moving but thought it would be easier to try it on speed two first. I am used to a mid-wheel drive powerchair, not a rear wheel drive one. My chair is more accurate and built for manoeuvrability. Whereas rear wheel drive ones offer more power. I had a bit of a whizz around the hall, and it felt different from what I was used to.

I felt that the chair itself was tough to control and the acceleration was far too quick, I spoke to one of the coaches, and they were able to adapt the control system of the chair. I felt that I was able to keep the speed, but the initial acceleration was easy to manage and didn't throw me around as much.

The first skill they set up was slalom. It felt quite easy on speed 2 and stable, so I turned it up to speed 3. The chair was very twitchy and quick. I found once the chair initially got going it was okay to steer in and out of the poles. It was just the start up that was very jumpy.

Dribbling a ball, which was about 2 feet in diameter, was a hard skill to learn and practice.

The chairs have a bumper around the front of your feet and at the back so you could push the ball going forward, and to pass the ball, you are meant to use the outside edge of the guard before the front wheels. When learning passing skills initially, I was hitting the ball with the left-hand side of the chair. I then discovered that one is meant to swing right and then quickly swing it to the left, so the momentum of the chair hits the ball. I found it was quite tricky to do, as when to moving the chair's position and I had to deal with the twitchiness of the chair and then swing around. I struggled with this at first!

The first team game we played was tennis. 2 teams outside of the line face each other, you have to hit the ball over the centerline. I found it gave me more chance to get used to the manoeuvrability of the chair. I was pretty good at blocking the ball, passing it to others and getting it over the line. The kids and the others were like pros. They were bombing around left right and centre. I was mainly using the front of the chair, but they were spinning around in circles and hitting the ball with the front, back and sides then spinning 270 degrees in what you'd think is the opposite direction, and then hitting the ball with some power.

Powerchair dodgeball was a great game. There were ten powerchairs speeding around the sports hall, most of them on full speed and the coaches kept throwing in balls. We had to dodge them and all the chairs. If a chair got hit three times, you were out. I thought this was absolute mayhem and really hilarious. The game was an excellent way of getting used to spatial awareness and how the chair performed. It was great fun.

At the end of the first session when people were getting out of their chairs. I tried it on full speed, and it was crazy. As soon as it accelerated the chair did a wheelie. They were mad, twitchy and sensitive. I felt like I was on a bucking Bronco, I was laughing my head off. Once it got going at full speed, it wasn't too bad to steer and manoeuvre, it was just getting started.

Slalom was a tricky skill to master, and the chairs are tough to drive in reverse! I did slow down the speed of my chair and found it was better to control. Sometimes I was physically pushing the golf ball with my knuckles and sometimes resting my hand on top of the golf ball. I found it easier to drive when my hand is cupping the ball, because this is how I operate my chair, but I can't always get my hand in position. I found this frustrating and challenging due to having no grip or useable function of my hands.

I did find afterwards that I was ever so dizzy. The movement of the chair jerking around battered my body and caused me a lot of aches and pains!

After going a few more times, I felt more comfortable with the powerchair and how it moved. Spatial awareness is critical, such as figuring out where other players are when the ball is coming and how to position the chair. I felt a lot more comfortable and confident driving the chair and controlling the ball at the same time. My main problem was trying to keep the momentum going on the chair. By constantly moving, takes away the jerkiness and twitching of the chair.

I struggle with getting tired quickly and my response time isn't always great, as I have to try and fight the spasm created by the chair. We adapted the chair and put a bit of drainpipe on the armrest. I found my arm was naturally sitting near the joystick instead of having to hold the weight of my arm. It made a huge difference and made it easier to control.

I had no idea how to play a proper game and what the rules were but was glad when I finally learnt them.

The rules are:
1. Each team is allowed four players on the court at one time, including the goalkeeper. A match lasts for two 20-minute periods.
2. "2-on-1". Only one player and an opponent are allowed within 5 metres of the ball when it is in play. If a teammate of either one comes within the 5 metres, the referee may call an infringement and award an indirect free kick. This forces the players to spread the field and prevents clogging up of play, allowing for a

greater free flow of play. The only exception to this violation is if one of the two teammates is a goalkeeper inside his/her goal area, then there is no infraction of the laws.

3. "3-in-the-goal-area". The defending team is only allowed to have two players in their goal area. If a third player enters the area, the referee may stop the game and award an indirect free kick to the opposing team.

In the case of either of these infractions (2-on-1 and 3-in-the-area), the referee may refrain from making the call if the player in question is not affecting the play. (Similar to the concept of the offside law in able-bodied football).

If there is intentional bumping or bashing, then this can incur a penalty. There are no throw-ins in powerchair football. Instead, you have to strike the ball with the front side of your chair.

I found it very tricky to combine all the skills and learn the rules, but it was great fun. You have to pay full attention to what's happening and where the players are and where the ball is.

Every week as an incentive, the sports club has an award for best player or most improved or best attitude within the session. I was delighted, one week, when I won the award for my reverse slalom. Reversing is very difficult in the chairs as they are very twitchy. When you are in a game, the tendency is to pull back to get out of the way which can be very jerky, so I was very pleased with myself when I was able to do the slalom in reverse with complete control. I like the idea of this award, and it was introduced into our S.A.N.D. sports club.

They have two different types of powerchairs at the club and I was starting to get the hang of the ones I had been using. The main problem I have with these chairs is maintaining power. When I go for a spin shot, I tend to swing the chair to the left and then when I rotate to the right to hit the ball, I tend to lose momentum and the ball doesn't go as fast as I want, this can be quite frustrating,
Team members mainly use the more expensive match chairs, which are £6000, but I was ever so pleased when they let me have a go in one. It took a while to get used to the chair as it was faster and had more power. I was terrible at reversing! I kept going forward to spin the chair around which meant I could not see what was going on, so they adjusted the settings which was great.

I found I was naturally sitting in a better position to push the controller and the difference in speed made it easier to get into attack mode. I also found it solved the problem of losing momentum when taking a spin shot, as the chair had a lot more power. The cage at the front is square instead of circular, so when making contact it gives the ball a good whack and gets it quite far across a court. The chair was so much more responsive, so it was easier to do the skills and overall a much more enjoyable experience. I felt I was able to get more involved in the game with the team. It's just a shame about the price!

I really enjoyed being involved in the game, however I felt as though the chairs were giving me too much of a beating each session and it was taking longer and longer for me to recover. Sometimes the fun factor doesn't outweigh the fact that I'm getting older and that I need more time to heal.

Powerchair football

12
HOSPITALS

Health is everything in life. I am now nearing my 19th year of paralysis, and I am amazed at the quality of my life and how many little problems I have had. When I was in the hospital, they scared the living daylights out of me warning me of autonomic dysreflexia, pressure sores, skin problems, general health problems and no end of complications that can often arise from spinal injury.

To say I have been lucky is an understatement, mainly due to the number of activities and places I have been to, where I have potentially put myself at risk, as mentioned throughout the book.

I have had minimal experiences with hospitals. I was requiring some physiotherapy a couple of years ago, and I had to speak to district nurses as I had fallen out of the system. They wanted me to see a spinal doctor for a checkup, so I went along to the spinal unit in Sheffield, where I was treated for eight months after my injury.

I went to do an M.R.I. to check if my spine was okay and for the doctors to give me a proper examination. Annoyingly, that day was a beautiful one, and I had to travel to Sheffield. What was even more annoying though was when I arrived at the M.R.I. unit they didn't have a hoist or any means of getting me out of my wheelchair. I was furious! Not only the fact that they didn't have the equipment, but more the fact that I am a tetraplegic with a high level of paralysis who needs assistance to get out of the chair and the whole point of the M.R.I. was to check my spine!

Luckily there was a spare appointment at another hospital where they did have the facilities, and they were able to hoist me out.
The only other time I have had an M.R.I. scan was directly after my injury and going into such a claustrophobic environment brought back all the first memories. Being in an M.R.I. machine is a horrible feeling. Your whole body vibrates and shakes due to the power of the scanner, and it felt like all my internal organs were moving around.

When I finally got a doctor's appointment, I went up to Sheffield spinal unit, and the doctors did kidney scans, blood tests and went over the M.R.I. They did a full cognitive test as apparently cognitive processing can diminish over time with spinal injury. Thankfully this has not been the case, as I have kept educating myself and I have good cognitive processing skills. They were looking over my notes, and I was delighted when they said that I had not been to the hospital in around 15 years.

The doctor said it was quite a rare case to have someone with such a horrid fracture never having any need to go back to the unit for any related issues, so I said I would see them in another 15 years.

I have very little to do with my G.P. He phones every now and again to check on my medication and see how my health is, but I have maintained a healthy lifestyle. Having a good care team over the years has undoubtedly improved my quality of life and helped keep me out of the hospital.

The only time in 18 years I have had to go back to A&E was when one of my carers took off one of my boots, and there was blood in the sock. She carefully took the sock off, and my big toenail was sticking up at 90°. We put a plaster on it and went to A&E.

The doctor did try and save the toenail although I wasn't bothered. I thought the best thing was to take it off. I decided to have a laugh with the doctor, but I don't think he saw the funny side. While he was taking off the toenail, I asked him if I would walk again. I could see the nurse behind him smirking, but the doctor didn't know what to make of my question.

He pondered on his answer for a couple of minutes and finally replied, "you do realise you are paralysed due to a high neck break." I don't know if he thought I was in denial or just genuinely didn't know how to respond. He thought I was deadly serious. You have to have a laugh when you can and look at the lighter side of life!

13
THE NEGATIVE CHAPTER

Life after spinal injury isn't all fun and games and cruises and safaris! Sometimes it is incredibly difficult to maintain a Positive Mental Attitude, and it can be challenging to find any joy, satisfaction or purpose.

Having people around 24/7 can be frustrating. Although they are there to help, which is much appreciated, having to put up with mood swings, issues and other people's problems can drive one crazy, and their input isn't always positive or constructive.

It's understandable that carers are going to come and go. We always agree on working a month's notice, which gives me time to find a replacement and complete training, when people leave on a positive note I do maintain friendships and often call them to see if they can help with a shift or I'll keep in touch by text or through Facebook.

I can remember hearing the door slam in the middle of the night and not hearing it re-open, which shocked me more than anything. I knew the carer had been drinking at work and had been arguing with her boyfriend outside earlier. She never took her car, so I knew I would have to see her in the morning. As luck would have it, I was due to go to my cousins 40th birthday in Bridlington the following day, so I arranged for someone to come in early. When I explained what had happened, he was shocked. She was not answering her phone or texts. Her car was parked directly behind mine, and I needed to go out. What was more shocking though, was the fact that she managed to take her car off my driveway without us knowing about it. She must have reversed the vehicle without turning the engine on, and we did not hear a thing. Suffice to say that was an instant dismissal!

I have had one carer who was on shift Monday night into Tuesday day, and she finished the shift. She then texted me on Wednesday morning saying that she was leaving the job. We had issues, but I thought they had been sorted out. I assumed I would see her for the next shift, but she had packed up all her belongings and food and just left. I had paid her until the end of the month and even paid her upfront holiday pay, but she just packed up and left without even saying goodbye. Leaving abruptly left the team with shifts that needed covering and funds low in the account. I felt hurt and angry, as it was someone, I had employed ten years previously. We had issues in the past, but I decided to give her another chance only to have it blown up in my face.

When I do employ, it is difficult to know exactly what I'm getting. Are they going to be capable and trustworthy? Will we get on? Will they be reliable? Can they do the job? Will they be able to handle money? Are they just putting up a front during the interview process? Are they going to be emotionally stable? I have to put my trust and faith in a stranger.

Often it takes time to get to know someone and reach the level of care as needed. Usually, it is frustrating, and I have to repeat myself over and over again and explain things over and over. There has only been one occasion where it hasn't worked, and we didn't get on. So, we both called it a day within the first few weeks. I'm generally a pretty good judge of character, but history has proven I don't always get it right.

Getting dressed and using the toilet is part of my everyday care. Sometimes it is so frustrating having other people wash and dress me. I accept it though, but sometimes it takes forever, and I want to get up and be ready!

Night times I generally sleep ok. Beer helps sometimes, but I try not to be dependent on it, which I was for a long time. I drank every night, but I realised it wasn't right for my health or weight. Having a drink is often a way of masking issues and helps numb some of the emotional pain. It became such a habit and routine; that was quite hard to break. I have never been a heavy drinker and four cans at night are usually the case. I mainly have this under control and have a drink on the weekends and throughout the week I have Kalms to help me sleep.

Some nights are terrible when I can't sleep, my mind works overtime. I do have carers staying overnight, but it's scarce that I shout for them. It is frustrating not being physically able to roll around to get comfy. The only thing I can move is my head. I can't even get up to have a glass of water. Nights do get very lonely and can seem to go on forever. Thankfully it doesn't happen all the time, and I do sleep very well.

Lack of physical intimacy is tough to take. It is something you get used to and learn to live without, I cannot even hug someone back, which can be challenging to accept, not being able to hug my Dad or Gill. I have tried dating sites, but it usually just feels awkward as soon as the chair or disability is mentioned.
It is hard enough sometimes maintaining four close relationships with carers. I never really realised at the start of the journey what a lonely road it was going to be, trying to retain and regain an independent

lifestyle. I do count my blessings that I have great support from my family and a handful of excellent friends who have been there through the years, especially Jay, Pro, Elk and Dave who have been there for me through thick and thin and just accepted that I am still me and we can always have a beer, a laugh and watch films.

Most evenings I have a couple of hours to myself before the next carer comes in which, gives me time to clear my head. I do go out a few evenings, but most evenings I have some time to myself.

It always has been, and I guess it will always be, a challenge to see people do activities I used to enjoy. It did take a long time to accept that there would be activities I could never do again. Friends also found it awkward talking about activities that I used to partake in. This is why I do challenge myself and do different activities. I have opened up a new world of events I never thought I would do.

One thing that is annoying is when things accidentally go walkabout. Somehow over the years, a name badge for my networking group went missing, a 3/4 full bottle of Fahrenheit fell in a bin and got lost, and a Berghaus fleece jacket got lost. Every winter I put all my best t-shirts away for the summer. They were placed in a black bin bag and stored but when summer came, they were nowhere to be found. I think they were somehow, sent to a charity shop.

Most things don't happen intentionally, but it was quite painful one morning when I got up and got ready to go to a business meeting where I made a bit of an effort dress-wise, and someone accidentally sprayed Fahrenheit directly in my eye. My eye was watering throughout the whole meeting. Just for the record, I don't recommend this.

I have built quite an independent lifestyle, but I do often feel like I am just observing my own life and having other people do things for me. At times it feels like life is just happening around me, people having kids and getting married and all that.

Month-to-month I generally do okay financially, but sometimes it can be challenging when something breaks, or needs fixing, or work needs doing, and it has to go on my credit card, especially things like my van and powerchair. I have to contribute towards my care costs, it was around £30 a week that is changing in the future to £85 a week, which is going to be a massive struggle financially. My house was in desperate need of redecorating, but I could not afford to do it, so it all went onto my credit card. Thankfully a solution presented itself to pay it off.

Money is a complicated thing to manage. I do all my banking by the Internet because I can't physically handle cash, which can be quite frustrating. There have been times over the years where amounts just haven't added up.

Although it is fantastic having time and freedom, sometimes it can be challenging passing the time and fighting the boredom. Especially when I don't have much on, I like to keep myself active and have projects on the go but sometimes it's not always the case, and this is when it's challenging to maintain self-esteem and confidence. I find it difficult to find things I can sometimes do and very difficult to find the motivation to do anything. It's tough to drag myself back to reality.

Not exercising or having physiotherapy has had a massive impact on my body over the years and the problems that I have had due to my disability and paralysis vary. The problem that I get in my arms is too much tension and too much spasm.

The limited amount of movement that I do have has become more challenging to maintain over time. I find it harder to do the tasks and jobs that I can do for example, using a computer or iPad or driving my powerchair. Due to the tension, these have become harder and harder to do for a more extended period. Driving my powerchair is essential, and it sometimes can be challenging to maintain the control and ability needed to control the chair. I find it can sometimes cause safety issues by trying to get my hand off the controller in time.

I have a lot of problems with my shoulders, which affects the movement and can quite often cause discomfort. I also have tension and stiffness in my back that is uncomfortable and can cause me a lot of stress. This affects my posture and my seating, I can see that I am hunched over quite a lot which causes unnecessary pain and discomfort in my back and neck. I have to fight to sit upright which affects my mood.

It causes discomfort when I'm hoisted out of the chair and lowered onto the bed. The initial impact can set me up into spasm until it relaxes, and my body can lie out straight. There is a lot of tension and stiffness in my legs, which causes me discomfort when sitting and affects my circulation that makes my legs and feet swell. Having this tension in my body also affects my carers when they are dressing me as it is harder for them to move me and put clothes on. It also makes it difficult for them to roll me. Sometimes it can be quite a battle for the carers trying to get a jumper or a jacket on me. Having this spasm and discomfort makes it really hard to rest at night. This makes it even worse for me to go out all day and drive the chair all day.

One way I find helps loosen up my body is by having a beer or two. This naturally increases health risks and means more chance of putting on weight. I did find a physio that is going to have a massive impact.

The one thing that gets on my nerves is not being able to scratch my head when it gets itchy. It drives me insane.

Society and the environment will always be a hindrance especially regarding access to a lot of places. People are always going to be negative, judgemental and ignorant to some disability needs. I have found over the years people, in general, have become more aware of disabilities due to the Paralympic games and TV coverage.

The best way I can sum up my disability is, it feels like being in a straitjacket and I am just trapped inside! Or like a T-Rex with tiny arms that can't reach it's prey.

14
TECHNOLOGY TO HELP IMPROVE QUALITY OF LIFE

When I first moved into my home in 2001, I was not able to operate any equipment. Not being able to answer the phone, turn over the TV, turn on lights or even answer my front door was incredibly frustrating, it is incredible how one can take these things for granted!

I had a system put in by Steeper that was very basic at first. By hitting a button, it would start an L.E.D. sequence off, and when I got to the function I wanted, I pressed the button again. For example, when I went down to TV mode and clicked select, the L.E.D. sequence would start again. Then I would go down to channel click choose and start the series again to turn the channel up or down, this was a prolonged system, but it worked, and I was able to control my TV, Sky, DVD and answer the phone and make phone calls.

At the time it was probably cutting-edge technology. A few years later the whole system was updated, and instead of an L.E.D. sequence, I hit a button that presses the symbol. The idea was the same, and this equipment gave me back so much independence. It was fantastic at the time.

As time goes on so does technology. I used to download TV and films and then transfer them back to a multimedia hard drive and then control it with the up, down, left and right system.

Eventually, I went to streaming systems, and I bought myself a new TV that I found I was able to control via an app on my phone. I was also able to control the Amazon fire stick through my phone.

In January 2017, I got a Hive heating system from my dad for Christmas. The system was great as I was able to set different timers for the heating. I was able to turn it on and off from my phone. I found this was great for my independence as I am always cold, and the old boiler system only had specifically allocated time slots for on and off. Setting a heating system to your requirements is something everyone takes for granted but it was something I lost for a while, it is great to be able to put my heating on when I am cold and to be able to set it up when I am due to come home.

Touchscreen technology for mobile phones and iPads has made my life so much easier. Although I don't have any control over my fingers, they are sticking out enough to be able to operate these devices with ease, as time goes on, I use a computer less and less and do everything from my phone.

Nowadays you can buy more things off the shelf instead of having to purchase specialised equipment. For example, the Amazon Echo or the Google Hub, these can be operated by voice or directly through your phone. I had been curious about these for a while, one of my carers was using the system, and she bought me an Amazon Echo for Christmas 2018 and an on or off plug to try. I set it up to turn my fish tank on and off and was amazed by its simplicity. We set it up so I could operate my Hive heating system by voice. I bought more plugs so I can turn everything in my living room on or off by voice, either individually or as a group with one command. I also bought light bulbs that can change colour and brightness, these are great for mood lighting, and I can turn my bedroom light on and dim it before I am ready to get up.

I subscribed to Spotify and can select my music and even set it as an alarm so I can wake up to whatever music I feel like. I can fix myself reminders as well as asking for information. I now have three units, 1 in my lounge, 1 in my bedroom and 1 in the carer's room as you can use them as intercoms and talk from room to room. A function I do like about the Echo is the fact that any books I have purchased on Kindle, will turn into audiobooks and be read to me. I also bought a video doorbell that you can operate by voice, but it was very temperamental and useless.

TVs can now be operated by voice. I don't tend to do that though, and I use the remote on my phone. The only thing I use my old system for now, is operating the bed in my bedroom. The whole system seems outdated now.

I used to have to rely on Dragon naturally speaking on my PC to be able to write down any content especially long sections and especially writing a book. The system was extremely accurate, and the more I used it, the better it became. However, now I have been using the microphone on my iPhone or iPad it is not as accurate as Dragon, but I can get the bulk of text down and then go back and tidy it up. I preferred the Dragon system however; it is easier to use tablets.

I find it does cause a lot of problems though, I do have to keep pressing the microphone button on, and it goes off after a certain amount of time, this can interrupt the flow of the work. The major problem with voice dictation on tablets is sometimes you write paragraphs and then when you go back and look at it a few days or weeks later, none of it makes sense, and it has written a complete load of jibber. I find sometimes it can be hard to think about what I wrote, and even more challenging for someone else. The majority of this book I wrote by talking directly into my phone.

I often find these appliances do save time and make life a lot easier and give me Independence. I do often see that when I make a voice command though that my carers will say, did you want something? Which counteracts the command and I have to explain I am talking to Siri or Alexa and then do it again. I guess they are that used to being asked, so sometimes I can't win.

Grammar has never really been my forte. I was told about some software called Grammarly, which was about $160. I was able to find it on eBay for a fiver to use someone else's subscription. It was easy to use and very helpful.

The Internet itself is a massive resource and a huge step forward for technology. It is so easy nowadays to find information on any subject. I purchased some video editing software called Movavi, which is an excellent piece of software and it is very good at editing. I can create images, add pictures to video and extract audio. I can get perfect quality videos from this, and I am also able to record podcasts that can be distributed via Spotify and other major platforms for free.

I think it is great that you can use these resources without being having to spend a fortune, this means I can get my message either verbally or written, out there without a massive outlay.

15
HELPING OTHERS

Helping people is something I like doing. I get a lot of joy and satisfaction by assisting others in one way or another.

When I first got involved in the S.A.N.D. sports club back in 2002, I had no idea the impact it would have on me. Initially, I had to do ten voluntary hours as part of the Community Sports Leader Award, and it started me on a journey of sports coaching and working with people with disabilities.

I realised the impact I would be able to have on children with disabilities, I understood that if they could see that I was able to maintain a quality of life and do physical activities then hopefully they would be able to look past their conditions and participate in sport.

Over the years I feel that I have had a significant impact on the club and its members, from running sessions, motivating and encouraging the children, to talking with and giving advice to them and their parents as they needed to see that their child is capable of having a quality of life despite having a disability. I have helped with fundraising for equipment for the club and done talks for the Inner Circle and W.I, who had both raised some money and helped with gear. I gave them peace of mind and knowledge that the money was being used to improve the club.

I have been heavily involved with both primary and secondary schools with refereeing Boccia for leagues and competitions over the years, which is something I enjoy, and it helps out by having someone who is available during the day who knows and loves the game. I also give coaching, motivation, praise, and tips.

While studying for my degree, I had to do 200 hours of practice with a wide range of clients and conditions. I have no intentions of breaking any confidentiality, but over the period, I helped with alcoholism, drug addiction, depression, child abuse, suicidal tendencies, separations, disability, and violence and anger issues, amongst other things.

I enjoyed the challenge of counselling and found it satisfying when the client had a breakthrough, but it was also extremely challenging and hard work. I often felt it was hard listening to and being there for someone empathically when I felt my problems outweighed theirs in my mind. For these reasons, I decided not to pursue it.

I met a chap at 4 Networking who in his 40-second introduction talked about his business transporting people to and from airports and venues. He asked to have a chat with me, and I agreed.

It turned out he runs a football club for children with cerebral palsy, which involves frame football. He asked me if I would go along to see what they did and talk to some of the parents about my own experiences, about life in general and my involvement in sports and disabilities.

One of the parents was struggling to cope with their child. The child who was only nine was struggling with his disability. I had a chat with both of them and gave them a different perspective that I hoped would made a difference.
The lady was telling me about how her son was struggling to come to terms with his disability and was always saying things like, why was I born like this? Why doesn't my body work as well as others? What did I do to deserve this? I don't want to live like this. I wasn't expecting this at all, and it completely threw me off guard, I felt as though I had to put on my

counselling hat. It was upsetting hearing the struggles they had and how the child felt.

I had a chat with the child about some of my limitations that I had overcome, and I told him about Positive Mental Attitude and that with the right attitude you can achieve anything and the impact that this has had on me in my own life.

I went back the week later but was running late and didn't get much time to spend with them. The lady caught my eyes straight away and said her child had been like a different child and that she was hoping to see me. She noted how all week he had been speaking with a Positive Mental Attitude– you can achieve anything! And she said for the first time he was looking forward to the club and had been optimistic and enthusiastic all week.

I said this to the child when he was on his own, and his mum wondered if it had come from me. I was pleased that I had made a significant impact with just a few select words.

On the way out, his mum thanked me and said she had been saying similar for years, but he always responded by saying, "You can walk! You have no problems…" To hear it from someone with my condition it had an impact.

I received a follow-up text a few days later from her saying all his teachers and learning assistants had noticed a massive change in his attitude and approach to everything and was wondering how such a shift in thinking had occurred. She said it was because he had met someone who had broken his neck and was a wheelchair user who had spent a short period with him and given him some kind words of encouragement.

I felt a real sense of accomplishment, achievement and pride for being able and willing to make a difference to someone's life.

I am certainly no expert in bringing up a child with a disability, but I have seen a lot over the years and gained a perspective from talking to the parents.

One of my carers, whose job is to help and look after me, spoke to me about some of his issues with money, motivation, relationships and not doing anything about it. After spending time with me and listening to one of my talks, he reflected on his problems and realised that he was thankful for what he had. He understood that if I can maintain a positive lifestyle and do things out of my comfort zone and get myself out of debt, then he should be doing more to help himself, work on his relationship and getting out of debt. To look forward to life's possibilities instead of dwelling on the past. It was quite rewarding to hear what a positive impact my talk had made on him and helped us move forward in our relationship as employee and employer, funny how roles can change!

One of our eldest S.A.N.D. members is Autistic, and it has been amazing seeing how he has grown and developed over the years, which is rewarding. He did some volunteering at Creswell Crags, it was great hearing what he was involved in each week, but college came to an end. His mum wanted to keep him in the position and was asking me how I went on with funding, accounts, payroll, and staff, etc. Dawn who has been my longest carer, literally from day one and is my senior team leader and sorts out our shifts and wages. I had a chat with her, she has known him for a while at the club and always made time for him. I was delighted when she said she would be interested in helping him two days a week on a Tuesday and Wednesday, but with our shift pattern, it didn't seem possible. We figured if we changed a couple of shift patterns, she would be able to do it. It meant that he had someone he already knew, and it gave her a new challenge. The impact she has had on him has been fantastic, the way he has grown and developed was well worth the hassle. If we hadn't been willing to adapt and change, I think he would have gone backwards not forwards in life!

During my time with Utility Warehouse, I have had to help lots of people regarding services and problems that do occur. I have never said the company is perfect, but they are very good at what they do. Part of my service, when someone joined as a customer was to take the hassle out of everything, and instead of having to phone through to head office, contact me first, and I would try and sort out problems, which is all part of the service. Sometimes they were problems I wouldn't be able to solve personally, and they had to go through to head office, but it certainly helped to speed up the process and take the stress out of things. It is always more personal when a customer has only one person to deal with. When people saw the business opportunity for what it was, I was always willing to help others and share tips and give advice, as there are a lot of things to learn. Talking to new team members and trying to guide them the best way, whether they did it or not was their choice!

My cousin is a 20-year survivor of cancer, and she said she was going to be involved in Relay for Life in York. A team was walking or running for 24 hours around a track. I said I would join in. I did a promotional video on Facebook about people I knew who had been affected by cancer which got about 500 views, and I was pleased with this as I am new to video marketing. Hopefully, a few people donated. It was raining heavily on the day, and people were camping overnight, I went for the afternoon and did about 15 laps and took a couple of videos for Facebook with a link to sponsor the team. It hit home talking to survivors, and it was good to do a couple of laps with my cousin. The team had a banner, and we were asked to write something on it. I wrote 'If you can survive cancer, you can survive a bit of rain.' Which turned out to be the team's motto and helped them get through what I imagine was a long, cold and wet night. I only stayed for the day.

I am well looked after personally financially, I have what is called a personal health budget, which used to be the Independent Living Fund, which enables me to live independently in my own home with the use of carers and have physiotherapy. Without this funding, my options would have been staying at a nursing home or living with my dad. I was asked recently to do a talk for a video for the council explaining my experiences and benefits due to the personal health budget, and the positive impact it had on my life. I saw this is a good way of giving something back and helping other people understand that there is a better option available.

By doing motivational talks about my life and my experiences and by my books I hope to create awareness about spinal injury and living with a disability and break down barriers and stereotypes about disability. The feedback I have been getting is great, and I am having such an impact and changing perceptions of disability. People are realising what they take for granted and how little issues may be blown out of proportion and holding them back.

I hope you the reader have been able to implement or change something in your own life by reading and understanding about the issues, obstacles, and challenges I have faced and overcome.

I feel if any aspect of my life journey and experiences can help someone else come to terms with their disability or lifestyle in general, then that is my role in life and hopefully over the coming months and years from meeting the right contacts, I can have an impact on a lot more people.

16
AFRICA

Visiting South Africa and going on safari was always a dream of mine that I never thought would become a reality. I had been talking to my dad for years saying that it was something I would like to do, he said to look into it and find out a price. The company I had travelled with previously did offer safaris for people with disabilities, but they seemed very expensive and explicitly stated they didn't have a wheelchair accessible vehicle.

I spent some time looking around the Internet and came across a video from a company called Epic Enabled, and the vehicle they took out on safari caught my attention straight away.

One of my carers at the time said it was something she wanted to do and told me her parents would pay for a holiday, so it started to seem more like a reality. While planning and looking into it, it was apparent there would be no hoists on the trip.

One of my friends also wanted to come, and we spoke about money. I said I would pay half and he would pay half so I would be guaranteed to have the muscle for lifting.

I mentioned this to my dad, and he said he and his partner would come along. I was ecstatic at this news; we started planning and paid for deposits, etc. Things happened with the carer, and it no longer became an option for her to come, and my friend's priorities changed, so I asked another one of my carers, who agreed to come. We decided we would use the money to cover the holiday, give or take a few hundred quid for doing it. I had the holiday booked about a year in advance, and there was no way I was missing it.

Eventually, the time came for packing, and I was hoping for an adventure. We drove to Manchester that was a two-hour drive and then we waited a couple of hours at Manchester airport and flew to France. I found the airport not letting me through the gate in my powerchair made this worse. They said I had to go through on the chair from the airport, which made no sense to me. I had to be lifted from one chair to the other in front of hundreds of people, and then we went to the gate only to sit there for 45 minutes in an uncomfortable plastic chair looking at my powerchair.

We had problems with my chair on the small plane due to the height of the backrest, and the whole backrest had to be taken off, so the chair could fit in the hold, that held up the plane, as the only person that seemed to be able to sort the chair out was the pilot.

We then flew from France to Johannesburg that was about an 11-hour flight and was horrendous for me. I felt so uncomfortable for most of the journey and was unable to get any rest. It was a fantastic take-off; it was so smooth that we didn't even know we had taken off. I may have had a maximum of an hour's sleep on the plane.

When we finally landed, and I was lifted from the chair on the plane to the aisle chair it became apparent that the gel cushion I was sitting on had folded over while I was being raised into the seat, which explained why I was so uncomfortable. On the plane, once you get relaxed, there is not a great deal you can do about it.

My Dad and Gill flew out separately, and we arranged to meet them in Johannesburg. The flight times were perfect as they landed about half an hour after us, so by the time we had had a cup of tea they were there. It is always quite a strange feeling when you arrange to meet someone on the other side of the world at an airport. I still find it reassuring when you get to an airport on the other side of the world and there is someone holding the board with your name on it.

Charles was our helper for the week, and he was fantastic. Alfie who ran the tour in the Epic truck picked us up at the airport. The truck was excellent, it was a Mercedes lorry, and the entire container had been opened up. It had three windows that were only plastic sheeting so they could be rolled up. It could have seated 19 altogether. There were seats at the front, and the back and wheelchairs went in the middle, there were clamps in place so the chairs could be fixed down and it had a hydraulic tail lift on the side of the truck to get in.

Thankfully we only had about a 20-minute drive to the first lodge and with it just being about 11 am we had all day to chill out.
A couple of people had a quick nap, but I was too excited and had a look around with my dad. The lodge was charming.

The truck was to-ing and fro-ing from the airport picking up more people, we were introduced to a young lad in a wheelchair from Belgium and a married couple from America, one of whom used a powerchair, and in the evening we were introduced to 2 more American ladies.

We had a briefing and a talk about what to expect from the tour and then had a disappointing, expensive meal and finally went to bed.

I had a terrible night's sleep. Even though I was exhausted, my back was killing me, and I woke in so much pain, probably from all the travelling.

I was quite worried about this and hoped it wouldn't affect my holiday of a lifetime. I kept dosing myself up with Nurofen for the trip, and thankfully this problem didn't persist.

We had a very early start and a horrible breakfast. I was surprised about the food there and was glad we weren't staying there long. It was at this point that we realised I was going on a safari for ten days and one of my carers had forgotten to pack any socks!

We all loaded onto the truck and started driving from Johannesburg to the Kruger. It was about an 8-hour drive with a couple of stops for dinner. Ironically, we stopped at a Wimpy because it was the only place that was accessible. I didn't get off the truck, but I was told that the garage/travellers rest area had a rhino in a small enclosure.

I was tired, and in discomfort, I had music on for most of the journey. I passed the time just looking at the beautiful scenery that was continually changing and it was stunning. I remember Olifants River that seemed to go on for miles and had the most beautiful waterfall. It was quite strange seeing all the poverty and families trying to make a living selling things by the side of the road. Seeing the state of some of the houses and villages was also quite upsetting.

We finally made it to Tshukudu Private Game Reserve where we were due to spend four nights. We were all shattered from all the travelling, but we had made good time on the journey and arrived at the park to find out the 4x4 Jeep was going out on a night tour in the next 15 minutes. We all agreed we wanted to be on it.

We were told that this game reserve didn't have accessible vehicles so I would have to be transferred, which was explained to us. They said that they would pull the truck right up next to the Jeep and use the tail lift to get the chairs on and then we would be transferred to the Jeep. Moving was quite a scary process, but thankfully no one was dropped. It was even worse in reverse doing it by spotlight and torches.

Within about 5 minutes we had spotted giraffes, and all the travelling seemed worth it. The ranger said one of the cheetahs was eating its kill; we drove to it and parked up by the side of the cheetah eating away on a freshly killed deer. It was quite a sight as we were metres away and it was quite breathtaking. We let it digest and then we went and found elephants and watched those as the sun came down, which was so red and beautiful.

It felt great to be seeing nature after having spent so much time travelling and being awake. I think this was probably the third day of the trip. We had our supper and then we all went to bed early, amazed by what we had seen straight away.

The next day we went for a walk with a caracal that was about the size of a fox and looked like a lynx. It was so friendly. The giraffes were quite happy just eating away. We went out for another evening tour and saw elephants, giraffes, buffalo, impala, and rhino. We parked the Jeep next to the rhinos, and they wandered up right next to us. They were that close you could hear their heartbeats, which were quite exhilarating. We were told to be very quiet and be motionless. I kept hearing a clicking sound followed by a winding sound. We found out later that this was the American ladies who had travelled all that way for the experience of a lifetime and all they had were rubbish disposable cameras. We had taken a video camera and expensive cameras; I sent a copy of my photos to the ladies in America once we arrived home. They were pleased with this, as the pictures that they had were rubbish.

Our camp was in the middle of the reserve, and when we got back from the tour, elephants were trying to get into it. The owners wanted to keep the reserve as tidy as possible, naturally for the tourists and there were lots of lovely fresh plants which the elephants wanted to eat, it was quite strange after going out on tour to come back to shoo off the elephants before we got into camp.

On the next day, we went for a walk with Floppy. He was called this because he had a floppy ear. He was the cheetah we had seen eating its kill. It was massive and such a beautiful creature, he let us follow him, and we stroked him and took lots of photos of him. While my dad was stroking him, he rolled over and caught him with his claw and left quite a mark. I felt quite nervous driving my chair so close to him so that I could stroke him. The last thing I wanted to do was catch a cheetah and run over its paws or catch its tail. He was hand bred but was still a wild animal. It was extraordinary being able to get so close to a beautiful large cat. I never thought in my wildest dreams that I would get to walk with a cheetah.

We had to get up very early and to say it was red hot would be an understatement. I think it was about 40 or 45 degrees. You could barely breathe, so it was nice to be able to chill out and relax back at the reserve.

We then took a drive out of the game reserve and went to meet Jessica the hippo. The location of the valley and the river was stunning. It was in the middle of nowhere. We sat and watched a video that told us about the hippo. She likes coffee and sweet potatoes.

She was found during the floods of 2000 and was still attached to her mother's umbilical cord. A man called Tony, who was a ranger, felt sorry for this one because her mother had died, but she was still attached, rescued the calf and he saved her.

We went to meet her, which involved reversing down a 50, or 60-degree ragged path that was horrendous. The slope was very narrow and rocky and wet and slippery. We had ropes tied to the chair with two people steadying the chair, that was quite hair-raising and very scary. We then had to get onto a floating jetty, which was probably an understatement. It was more like a floating raft that didn't particularly feel very stable anyway but was even less stable when a giant hippo was trying to get out of the water.

First, everyone fed her apples and I moved my chair very carefully towards the edge of the jetty. It was initially very frustrating, as I couldn't entirely lean down far enough to be able to stroke her. When she came onto the dock for a drink, she was bottle fed cold tea, and she loved it. I had another go, and I was able to stroke her. The American guy on our tour didn't look like he had any legs, he did, but he was sitting on them. He was quick to stroke her and seemed very worried. It wasn't until I watched the video when I got home that I realised he had undone his belt around his chair. He was only a tiny man, and he had lent over the side of his chair so he could stroke her. It looked like he could have just fallen inside of her and been her dinner.

Then people kissed her on the nose, and I got to stroke her face. It was like looking into the mouth of a dinosaur, but she had such lovely, loving, friendly eyes and you could look straight into her soul. I had never experienced anything like this, it was so emotional being at one with such a large creature.

She then had a back massage from people's feet. She spent half her time interacting with other hippos in the wild so was free to come and go as she pleased. The rest of the time she interacted with humans and watched TV and liked classical music.

For me, this was one of the highlights of the safari. It wasn't just about getting close to a hippo that was breathtaking. It was about all the obstacles that it took to get down there, and it made me realise that as a paralysed powerchair user, if you can get down to the bottom of a river bed and stroke a hippo it changes your opinion of boundaries. If this can be achieved there really are no limitations. I always remind myself of this experience when I feel I am struggling, or I can't see the light. I think to myself, remember the time you got to the bottom of a riverbed and stroked a hippo!

I quite often tell this story, and people think that when I talk about a hippo, I am talking about a baby or a small animal, which was not the case at all, she was maybe 8 feet long and 3 feet wide, and her teeth must have been 8 to 10 inches long. She was a beast!

We also saw lions and leopards in sanctuaries at the game reserve, which were more for educational purposes and could not be released back into the wild.

We spent four nights at the private game reserve getting up close and personal with nature, and I wondered how Kruger National Park could come close to such an experience. It was a completely different experience being in the Kruger Park.

The Kruger National Park is enormous, and we moved around to different camps. The scenery was breathtaking, and we stayed in Alfie's truck while in the Kruger, so we were limited to which roads to go through. Which was great because my chair was strapped down and I had a belt. We were able to roll up all the plastic sheeting on the windows, because of the heat, we had open windows, and it was like going through a Safari Park on a vast open moving platform. We saw herds of elephant and rhino up close, and a pride of 7 lions walked in front of the truck. The male was especially suspicious of us, and we saw lots of cubs too.

We saw a very rare black rhino. My carer and I were very lucky and privileged to see a wild leopard fighting with baboons early in the morning. We saw some stunning birds, trees, plants and amazing sunsets.

The company we travelled with was excellent and catered for all my needs, apart from having a lift, but human resources were supplied. The tour host had a great trust system where every time you helped yourself to a beer or soft drink you put a tick on a sheet. To my knowledge, not one person took advantage of this and abused it. I would rather pay as I drink, as I am partial to a beer or 3.

The evening meals were freshly prepared, and we had a good breakfast and a snack for dinner. There was a real sense of camaraderie and friendship with everyone eating together.

The end of it shattered us, as we were the last to bed every night and first up every morning. I had been lifted, battered and bashed around and had some bruises for a few weeks afterwards.

The journey home was horrendous. We all had different flights and different times and ours was the latest. Everyone had to travel together in the truck to get back to the airport that was about an 8 or 9 hour drive. We had to wait around the airport for about 7 hours without a single penny to our name. I think we had just enough to buy a meal each and we had to share a cuppa.

We then had the main flight from Johannesburg to France, which was about 11 or 12 hours. I had more problems at the airport, because they put me on a small slippery unsuitable wheelchair that I kept slipping off. We then had a couple of hours to wait for our last flight from France to the U.K. We managed to blag first class which was great as I had more legroom, and it was easier for the crew to lift me on.

I was so tired that I just passed out. I managed to get half an hour's sleep, and during that time I missed out on the champagne, and good food, which I was told was lovely. We arrived back at Manchester, and we were the last people off the plane because they had taken the back off my chair again so it could sit in the hold. I was perched on an aisle chair, and the crew had the cheek of bringing up my powerchair with the back unattached and told us to sling it and clear away so other people could get on the plane. We had no tools and were very tired. How we were expected to fix my chair and move me on the aisle chair, and powerchair in 2 bits was a joke. We were both fuming!

I refused to be moved until they fixed my powerchair and got me in it. People were trying to get on the plane and getting frustrated, but they could see the situation and eventually engineers had to go and get spanners and fix my chair. We then had to drive home from Manchester. I think it took about 36 hours in total without sleep to get back.

The holiday was an experience of a lifetime, and I will never forget it. It made me believe that the only limits we have are the ones we set ourselves.

Meeting and feeding a hippo

Me, Wayne and Floppy

17
NORWAY

Seeing the northern lights had been a goal of mine for a few years, I decided to start looking into the possibility of going somewhere to see them.
I started looking around on the Internet to find accessible places I could go to. Initially, I wanted to go to Iceland, as I knew it was one of the best places in the world to see them.

I made enquiries and was shocked by the price to get there, even just for a few days. I looked into Greenland, but it wasn't accessible. I also came across a flight where you could get on a plane and hope that you saw the lights.
I felt this didn't appeal to me, as there was no guarantee. I wanted a full experience.

From my previous travels, I have had to endure a lot of discomfort from flying. From being lifted and using airport wheelchairs to being worried about my powerchair being abused or dropped while flying.
I set myself a goal in January 2015 to see the northern lights, and I knew I needed to set myself a goal to get through the hard times of my Utility Warehouse business, so I started putting my commission away

into a savings account each month, which gave me a goal and a reason to do the business.

I came across a cruise leaving from Southampton on March 8, 2016, going to Norway. I had read this would be a perfect time of year and an excellent location actually to see the lights.

By the time I had come across this holiday, I had enough to cover the deposit. It was then a case of putting money away each month for about a year to be able to pay for the cruise.

Adam was very interested in this opportunity to see the lights with me, so my care was sorted. I mentioned to my dad that I had booked the cruise and after a couple of days to my surprise and joy he decided to come along with his partner.

When the time finally came to pack my bags, I was very excited but unsure we would get to see the lights due to them being a natural phenomenon. I prepared myself by getting proper winter clothing. I bought a North Face down jacket, skiing trousers, fleeces, walking boots, etc. I imagined it was going to be cold and I wasn't going to be let down just by lousy clothing. My carer's wife who is a teaching assistant made me laugh when she commented: "where does he think he is going? Into the Arctic?" Which was precisely where we were going!

When we first arrived at the port, I was very excited to see the size of the ship that was called The Oriana. It was very different from the little dinghies I was used to.

It was great to get on board the vessel after driving to Southampton and seeing how luxurious and posh the cruise ship was. It was terrific. It took some getting used to, and we kept losing each other at the start.

I found the ship was fantastic for access and I was able to come and go as I pleased and went into shows, theatres and the cinema. I enjoyed this aspect more than I expected. I also saw a comedian, a flautist, a cellist and a fascinating set of talks, including a police officer telling her stories as a female officer in the 70s. I soon got to know the waiters, and they got to know my situation. I just had my cabin card sticking out of my wrist supports, so they were able to sort out drinks and anything else.

I had hired myself a hoist. It was essential as I was going with one carer and a shower chair that we found we were unable to use as the size of the shower room was tiny. There was no way my carer could move around to shower me in such a small space. I had looked into hiring a bed for the 12 days duration, but the price was costly at £440. I couldn't justify it at the time, in hindsight it was necessary.

The first night we used pillows to support my back. I think the first couple of nights I was okay, but when we hit the North Sea, and I had problems staying on the bed.

It wasn't the easiest thing to sleep on anyway with the motion, but I had a couple of nights where I woke up, and my body was diagonal across the bed with my feet hanging over the side. One night I ended up in a pile of pillows against the wall, and I wasn't able to wake my carer up. If I had been on the opposite side of the room, I would've ended up on the floor.

We ended up keeping the sling under my body, attached to the hoist with a little bit of tension across my shoulders to keep me in bed.

The first place we moored at was called Andalsne. The first thing we saw when we looked out of our cabin window was a fantastic mountain. Once we had finished breakfast surrounded by stunning scenery, we were able to get off the ship and have a look around.

Having not seen snowy mountains since about 2003, this was a beautiful thing to wake up to, and the fjords were breathtaking. Right next to the dock was tourist information and the first thing most people did, including myself, was to log onto free WIFI and let family and friends know we were okay. It's funny how times have changed! I liked this place it was quaint and picturesque.

We then went further north and stopped at Tromso, which was a nice place to see. It was just a small town. We went to an art gallery that did not impress me. There were some stunning 18th-century oil paintings of mountains, fishing villages, etc, but there was a lot of rubbish that I could have painted.

There was, however, a two-mile bridge across a fjord with an Arctic cathedral at the end, which was freezing to cross but it had a fantastic view. It was undoubtedly a fair trek across it, and I was glad I was able to get a bus back. It did make me laugh though as my carer had decided to not come into the museum, which was probably the right decision and when we met up with him again, we said we were going to cross the bridge. His face sank, as he had just been all the way across there and back. The weather wasn't that great, and he was freezing.

We then headed to Alto that is at the top of Norway. There were some lovely ice statues here, and the snow was compact enough to drive on. I had some fun getting to full speed and banging the chair left and right so it would slide.

We were fortunate as it was just going in to summer and everything was starting to thaw. We went back the day after, and most of the statues were starting to melt. It was ever so scary travelling on the bus as my chair was sliding around. We decided to get off and go to a different museum, it was Sod's law that the one afternoon my carer chose to stay on the ship, we got off the bus and the ground was starting to thaw out. I was with my Dad and Gill, and it was cold, wet and windy, and the chair was sliding everywhere, and I had no control of it whatsoever. My dad had to steady and push the chair and guide me back, so we didn't make it to the museum. When we got back to the bus stop, people commented on how they saw a struggle between a 70-year-old man and a large powerchair, I don't know why no one came to help.

For days there was speculation as to whether we would see the northern lights. They were offering excursions for at least £160 per person, I felt this was expensive so didn't do anything for a few days. By the time I had decided that I wanted to go on an excursion all of the accessible ones had sold out.

We were spending two nights here and knew this was the best chance to see the lights. They were estimated to be visible between 8 pm & 4 am so the plan was to stay out as long as possible. We had heard that the tours were only going about 15 minutes away from the ship to get away from the harbour lights, we spent the evening at the back of the boat where there was a bar and a designated smoking area where we had met with friends and had some great evenings.

It was a cloudy evening, so we sat outside drinking and waiting with a few beers, hot chocolate with Baileys and mulled wine because it was so cold. We could see green colours behind the clouds, so we knew something was happening. It was just a bit of a waiting game to see if the clouds were going to clear. The mood and feeling on the boat completely changed instantly, and there was a real feeling of euphoria in the air.

It got to around 9 o'clock, and the skies began to clear. At first, it was just little bits of light, and the first one I saw was like a zip opening in the air. At this point, I didn't know what to expect after all the anticipation and all the waiting; all of a sudden it was worth the wait. The sky just lit up in a mass of greenish yellowish light, dancing in the air. The lights never stayed the same and were continually changing and growing and moving around the sky. They were mainly like green droplets although there were tinges of orange and red.

Some lasted a few seconds whereas some seemed to build up and up and then explode into a mass of green in the sky. Some were like wisps, and some were like spirals, and some were just like explosions of mainly green, lighting up the sky. Some of them were even like curtains opening and as the curtains opened, more and more colour expanded. It's difficult to say how large and what kind of distance they covered in the sky, but it was undoubtedly vast. I would describe them as mystical and magical, and it was like a glimpse into heaven.

We saw the lights for about an hour, and they were spectacular and breathtaking! I was pretty gutted that my Dad and Gill didn't get to see them as they were in one of the theatres and by the time, we saw them it was over.

A lot of people didn't get to see them for various reasons, and some other people that had paid to go on excursions didn't get the timing right. There were some exciting conversations the morning after. Some people had a spectacular view, and some people just didn't and were disappointed. We were truly blessed to be at the right place, at the right time, which just happened to be at the back of the ship.

I read that every northern culture has legends about the aurora. One Inuit myth holds that the lights of the north are torches held in the hands of spirits seeking the souls of those who have just died, to lead them over the abyss terminating the edge of the world. Another holds that the lights are the visible spirits of unborn children playing ball in the heavens. (I got this from a photo from the museum).

It was a fantastic thing to see, and there were a couple more sightings afterwards but not as spectacular. Seeing the northern lights was a dream come true and it was everything I'd hoped for and had expected.

I am no scientist, but it is essential to explain what the northern lights are.

WHAT ARE NORTHERN LIGHTS?
The bright dancing lights of the aurora are collisions between electrically charged particles from the sun that enter the earth's atmosphere. The views are seen above the magnetic poles of the northern and southern hemispheres. They are known as 'Aurora borealis' in the north and 'Aurora australis' in the south.
Auroral displays appear in many colours although pale green and pink is the most common. Shades of red, yellow, green, blue and violet have been reported. The lights appear in many forms, from patches or scattered clouds of light to streamers, arcs, rippling

curtains or shooting rays that light up the sky with an
eerie glow.

WHAT CAUSES THE NORTHERN LIGHTS?
The northern lights are the result of collisions between
gaseous particles in the earth's atmosphere with
charged particles released from the sun's atmosphere.
Variations in colour are due to the type of gas
particles that are colliding. Oxygen molecules located
about 60 miles above the earth produce the most
common auroral tone, a pale yellowish-green. Rare,
all-red auroras are created by high-altitude oxygen, at
heights of up to 200 miles. Nitrogen produces blue or
purplish-red aurora.

The connection between the northern lights and
sunspot activity has been suspected since about 1880.
Thanks to research conducted since the 1950s, we
now know that electrons and protons from the sun are
blown towards the earth on the 'solar wind.'
The temperature above the surface of the sun is
millions of degrees Celsius at this temperature;
collisions between gas molecules are frequent and
explosive. Free electrons and protons are thrown from
the sun's atmosphere by the rotation of the sun and
escape through holes in the magnetic field. Blown
towards the earth by the solar wind, the earth's
magnetic field primarily deflects the charged particles.

However, the earth's magnetic field is weaker at either pole and therefore some particles enter the earth's atmosphere and collide with gas particles. These collisions emit light that we perceive as the dancing lights of the north (and the south).

The lights of the Aurora generally extend from 80 kilometres (50 miles) to as high as 640 kilometres (400 miles) above the earth's surface. (https://www.northernlightscentre.ca/northernlights.ht ml)

I wanted to see the Ice Hotel while I was in Norway, as I knew it would be an once-in-a-lifetime experience. During the first visit to town, we arranged with the local tourist information to book an accessible taxi to take us there and were given a price and time the following day.

When we turned up, there was some confusion about myself being in a powerchair even though I spoke to the person face to face the day before and they wanted twice the money. We agreed to pay and were taken about half an hour into rural Norway only to find that the pathway to the hotel was very mushy. Although the chair would've got through it. The owner of the hotel wouldn't let me in for fear of me churning up the floor, which was annoying but understandable, so I sent my carer in to take some photographs.

I was pretty gutted at not being able to get in the ice hotel myself, but at least I can say I did make it there. I would not have liked to be responsible for causing any damage to such a beautiful thing.

On the way back to the U.K. conditions were terrible and there was one particular night it was horrible on the ship. This night was made better though by winning a bottle of wine doing an Only Fools and Horses quiz, lubbly jubbly!
During the cruise, we met some lovely people, including two models that we ended up spending most of our evenings with, which was great fun. P&O was brilliant, and at the end of the cruise, they left us a set of coasters with pictures of the northern lights on and a certificate saying we crossed into the Arctic Circle on March 12th at 11-40 am.

It was a fantastic experience, and I had no stress, no worries about my chair or the fear of being dropped. I felt cruising was the way forward.

Me. Dad and Gill and the Oriana

Me in Norway

18
SUMMER CRUISES

After the success of seeing the northern lights and realising how good and accessible cruise ships were, I instantly wanted to go back and have a summer cruise. I enjoyed the winter one, but I felt a little claustrophobic being inside the ship all of the time.

Going on a cruise ship is so much easier than having to mess around with planes and airports. Where I have to be lifted onto aisle seats from the wheelchair and put in airport wheelchairs that are usually ridiculously small for me. I don't have to worry about how my powerchair is being treated and whether or not it will fit into the hold without being dismantled.

When I got home, I phoned P&O, and they told me about a 7-day cruise leaving from Southampton stopping at France, Spain, and Guernsey. I booked it for the following summer. This time I decided to hire a proper bed with sides after the farce in Norway of nearly falling out of bed all the time, it was good to be comfortable on holiday in bed.

When the time finally came, I was looking forward to it. The previous week in the U.K. had been roasting, at about 30 degrees. I packed all my summer gear, including a couple of pairs of trousers for the evenings and a fleece. Wayne was up to the task of a week on a cruise ship.

Setting off to Southampton, the weather was great, and the first day at sea was quite lovely. I had a mad panic the very first morning on the ship though, when I got into my powerchair it wouldn't turn on. I had been having problems with it a few months before, so we changed the batteries and the electronics for the controller, and it was working fine. Thankfully it only did it once, and the powerchair worked for the rest of the holiday.

The first place we docked was in La Rochelle in France. Getting on and off the ship via the gangway proved very difficult as the walkway was very steep. It had ruts, every foot or so to stop people from slipping, but it didn't help the wheelchair very much.

The bus journey into town was about half an hour, and there were two spots on the bus for wheelchairs. The bus was already quite full which meant that I couldn't position myself in line with the direction of the coach, so I had to sit at an angle, and when the bus went around the roundabouts, the chair slid around everywhere, so Wayne had to hold onto the back of the chair for support.

La Rochelle was a nice quaint spot, and the weather was lovely. We had a wander around then sat and had an ice cream. We then went into a fantastic aquarium, although we were a little rushed for time.

When it was time to get back on the ship, the crew had to lift my chair up the first ramp because it was so steep, and three other people had to push me up while I tried steering and avoiding the ruts.
Two of them were just general crew but one of them was quite official looking, he was effing and blinding behind me saying it was my responsibility to check that I could get on and off okay. His attitude was terrible, and I was going to say something when I got to the top, but by the time we got in the ship and gone through security, he had gone.

At the front of the ship on the top level is what is called the crow's nest. The crow's nest is a charming posh-ish place in front of the boat and where you can get a magnificent view of the ocean and ports. Quite a lot of people sit in this area as it is usually quite quiet or occasionally a piano would be playing.
Unfortunately for me, I sat facing forward with my carer on the left of me, and as I was talking to him, his eyes nearly popped out. He said that directly opposite him was one of the dancers who had taken her jumper

off and had forgotten she didn't have a bra on so, he got a good view of some cute dancer's boobs while I was staring out to sea!

We then headed towards Spain and the weather completely turned. We had thunder and lightning, and about 6-metre swells and 20-foot waves. I found this didn't make the journey comfortable as the ship was rocking around everywhere. I felt okay while I was in the chair and I felt quite stable, but when I laid down and went to bed; it was very rocky and uncomfortable. We didn't get to see much of Santander due to the weather although we did get off for an hour or so and got a fridge magnet for my collection.

We did get off the ship at a port called La Coruna, which is a lovely place. But it was pouring down with rain. Across the island, there was a beach we had seen pictures of, and we were determined to get to it. I had to drive my chair around the bumpy corridors and streets in the pouring rain. The beach was lovely and idyllic and wholly deserted due to the storm. It was such a shame to find such a beautiful spot but not to be able to sit and relax there because of the weather.

We also couldn't get off the ship in Guernsey due to the bad weather. I had already been told I wouldn't be able to get off because they were tendering, which meant you had to get into a small boat to get to the port. A lot of people were quite upset and annoyed that they couldn't get off, as the water seemed quite calm. When I got home and spoke to my dad, he said he was planning on being in Guernsey at the same time as I was and surprising us. Luckily, he didn't, as he would've had a surprise seeing the Oriana just sat there in the middle of the ocean with no one getting off.

Most of the cruise was great; we met loads of great people, saw some shows, watched some films, did some quizzes and drank beers.

It was just a real shame as I was hoping for a summer cruise and we didn't get much chance to sit outside or enjoy much of the beautiful weather or enjoy the locations we went to, but these things are sent to try you. A lot of people were complaining and moaning that they had had a terrible cruise and a terrible holiday just because of the weather. It all comes down to attitude. We had a great time regardless!

I came back and instantly booked another cruise on a bigger ship called the Azura which was in May and went to Portugal, Tenerife, Spain, Lanzarote, and Gran Canaria. Cruises are great for sitting around and relaxing, and I spent a lot of time staring out to sea writing and editing this book.

When driving down to Southampton for this cruise it was a fantastic sight and sound, hearing and seeing millions of pounds worth of supercars driving down the motorway, Ferraris, Porsches, Lamborghinis, etc. It was amazing.
The Azura was a lovely ship and was a lot larger than the previous one I had been on and had great entertainment and food. The cruise ship was a lot more stable and the cabin larger.

I was ecstatic when we had dolphins swimming alongside the ship, and this was something I always hoped I would see. On the way back we managed to see a whale, which was great. I enjoyed Madeira. It was such a beautiful place with vibrant flowers and colours everywhere, and the view from the cable car over the mountains was spectacular. Lanzarote was lovely, and it was nice to have wheelchair access on the beach. La Palma was great having wheelchair access over the black beach. We generally got off the ship for 4 or 5 hours and just wandered around the ports and beaches stopping for a beer and an ice cream and of course to find a fridge magnet for the collection, which is coming along nicely. I have filled the fridge and started on the freezer now. My goal is to fill that too.

People are so friendly on ships, but I did have one time when I was about to leave a lift, and an elderly lady with a frame barged her way into it. I explained I needed to get out, but she was not having any of it, she ended up getting her frame caught on my chair, and I had to try and get out of her way and then move to get out of the lift, which took some doing!

The weather on this cruise was lovely and hot which was great. I opted for freedom dining, which meant you could eat at various restaurants and at different times, which meant I got to dine with different people at every meal. I didn't bother with the black-tie nights as I find them pretentious and it's not really me. On these evenings we ate at the buffet, in shorts, t-shirts and comfort! I was allowed to sit in the dining areas in my shorts, but my carer had to put jeans on, which made me laugh!

Our cabin was a good size to move the hoist, shower chair, and powerchair around but we didn't have a window cabin and were more central. It made terrible creaking and groaning and rattling noises. I think we were either near the kitchen or laundry as we could hear trollies clunking and grinding which meant restless nights and because we had no natural light, time was very disorientating and confusing.

I am not a racist person at all. Skin colour makes no difference to me. We are all just humans having an experience. However, P&O employs people from Goa, India, Bangladesh, and the Philippines, to serve food and drinks, do maintenance and do most jobs. They are on the ships for months at a time, and it's an excellent job or career for them as they can send money home to look after their families. Most are extremely helpful and friendly. Some are not and haven't got a clue what you are asking them! The first time I cruised I found it unsettling, as I felt it was a step back in time where the white race was superior using different races as slaves to cater to the white rich hierarchy!

One night we left a bar, and my chair was pulling to the left and grinding a motor, which was red-hot, and it was a worry for the whole trip. The chair felt fine on deck but struggled with getting on and off. The easiest way was to disengage the motor and use human resources to push my powerchair and me at a combined weight of 250 kg.

We were able to get off everywhere and see Gran Canaria, Spain, Lanzarote, Tenerife, and Portugal but unfortunately, my chair completely died at the last port and would only turn left and had to be pushed around the island back to the ship. Thankfully it was the final port. It just meant I had to be pushed around for a couple of days. Ironically the thing I love most about cruising is not having to worry about my chair being bashed or dropped while flying, and it went and died on me.

I am pleased that after three cruises I have never been sick on board, which surprises me after alcohol and all the motion. I am fine with the movement when seated but when I lay flat on my back it's a different story.

I did come back from this cruise full of cold and coughing up horrible stuff due to the air conditioning. Three thousand people together and temperature changes are just part of the price you have pay for these experiences! Incredible how a few days earlier, I was in amazing spirits seeing the world in beautiful weather without a care in the world and then, no powerchair and home feeling so run down. Oh well, worse things could have happened at sea.

The Azura

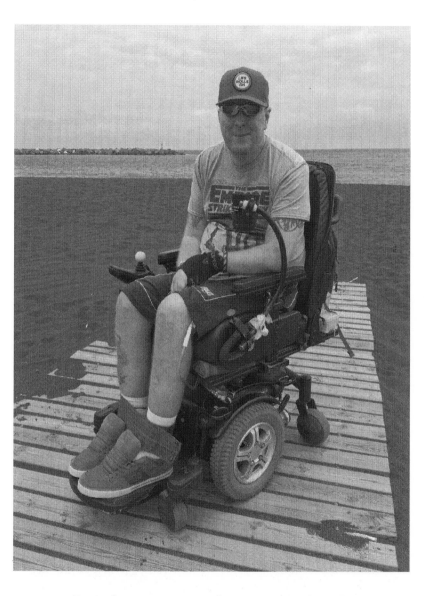

Lovely to get near the sea, on a beach

19
LONDON

A place I had always wanted to visit was London. I have been to Wimbledon, and I went to see the Olympics in 2012 but had never just seen the city.

I decided to go for the day, and the easiest way was to jump on a train and rely on public transport. No problems with getting on a train, and we just had to tell them I needed wheelchair access, so they got out a ramp that all trains have stored inside.

We arrived in London at Kings Cross with no problems. We had booked a ticket previously for the London Eye which worked out well as it was cheaper, as my carer got in free, which meant we just split the difference.

We had looked at the underground, but not all of the stations had lifts. So, we decided the best way to get around was with a combination of buses and on foot. We figured as we didn't have much time it would be best to head to see the museums first.

I enjoyed the Natural History Museum, and they had some fantastic exhibits. I was surprised by the size of it, and since we were on a timescale we had to get around as quick as we could which was a shame, I like to sit and read about the exhibits and to be able to absorb everything.

When we found the bus we should be on, the coaches themselves were great as we just told the driver I was in a wheelchair and they automatically sent out a ramp that was built into the doorway, and I just sat in a dedicated spot.

The first bus we got on pulled over and told us we had to get off due to a protest. I had no idea why! We got off, and it was difficult to find a connecting bus that we needed. We spent most of the day getting on and off buses, and this made it a great way of seeing the city and the architecture, the cars, the women and some of the sites.

One of the bus drivers wouldn't let me on and got quite argumentative and started shouting that I couldn't get on because there was a buggy in the wheelchair bay which there wasn't. He got quite angry, and my carer and people in the queue had a good go at the bus driver, until he eventually let us on.

We seemed to spend a lot of time on foot going around in circles, as everywhere we wanted to be, steps greeted us. Public transport was fine. London itself was one of the worst places I have come across for wheelchair access.

We decided it would be easier to get a taxi to take us to the London Eye; we had booked our tickets but went to the fast track office instead of the main information office. And although we had a specific time to go on, they barged us through all the crowds of people and straight to the front. We went practically straight on! Sometimes there are advantages of being a wheelchair user and people are amicable and helpful and help get you to the front of queues.

The views from the London Eye were spectacular, and it was great to be able to see all the sites such as Buckingham Palace, Westminster, Big Ben, Tower Bridge, etc. I thought it was quiet and a weird sensation going on the big eye, you certainly get a different perspective of London than just what I had previously seen on TV. I was pleased we made an effort to go and see the city.

We had a good walk around Big Ben and the Houses of Parliament. The architecture was stunning, although there was a strange atmosphere around the place as it was the week after Brexit and there were lots of camera crews and paparazzi about.

The day was exhausting, driving around on bumpy cobbles and uneven surfaces and trying to dodge people. We decided the best thing was to get a bus back to Kings Cross and get something to eat there so we would have plenty of time to catch our train home.

We found the street directly across from Kings Cross, but every restaurant had a step. I stayed where I was, and Wayne went to look around to find somewhere to eat. He came back having found a place to get a pizza that was accessible.

We were at a junction and instead of being able to cross over, due to no access. We had to pass 3 or 4 sections of the road to get to the other side. We were both over exhausted and hungry, but my carer said that the restaurant was on the other side of the junction and just up the road, it took me a little longer to cross all three sections, so I lost him. I assumed I had to drive up a hill. I started driving up thinking I was following him and that he was ahead of me. I had a cap on so wasn't able to see that far ahead, and I was tired and struggling to drive, but I soon realised I could not see him. I kept thinking to myself, do I go further up or back down.

I asked a lady if she knew where the pizzeria was, and it was further down, so I had gone too far, but he wasn't there. He had tried to phone me and wasn't sure where I was. I didn't hear the phone ringing, and because of my disability, I would not have been able to answer the phone anyway. It was in my rucksack (because I can't hold my phone, I would have it strapped to my leg under normal circumstances). I had to ask a stranger to get my phone out of my bag; my phone and wallet are usually kept in the same pocket of my rucksack. I phoned him. It turned out the restaurant was right near the junction where we had started. We managed to keep track of each other all day in central London but somehow lost each other on what I thought was a straight road. It's not a nice feeling losing your carer in London while you're in a wheelchair. It was a little bit disconcerting for us both, but luckily, we were not that far from each other, but when that initial panic sets in, it's not good.

We did laugh about it, over our well-deserved pizza and a beer and once we had eaten, it was obvious where we had lost each other.

I was glad when we were back on the train and on our way home. Annoyingly, when we booked tickets the cost and time was better to go from Doncaster, not Retford. I was gutted when the train stopped in

Retford, but the van was in Doncaster, so we had to go and get the vehicle and then come home. To top it all off my carer lived in Doncaster, which meant he had to drive back.

I enjoyed the experience, and I'm glad I got to see some of London, but it was far too chaotic, manic and stressful.

Big Ben

20
U.W.

When I joined Utility Warehouse in 2013, I had every intention of making it work. I do believe it is a solid business with fantastic services and residual income is a tremendous way to build a better life, and it really can make a difference to a lot of people involved. I love the idea of getting paid over and over again for doing a job once. I love the concept of network marketing. By building a team you can earn a small percentage of each team member's customer base, so in effect, you are getting paid from people you don't know and from customers you have never met.
So far, it's been an extraordinary journey with lots of ups and downs!

Initially, I attended every training session and every meeting I could. Some of these meant travelling quite a distance, but I felt it very important to throw myself in completely.

The first couple of years went very well, and I started gathering customers myself and started building a team. I had great support from Adam Barr, who was an old friend of mine who introduced me to the opportunity.

I engaged with the system and improved my knowledge and understanding by reading and listening to the books not just about the company itself, but I studied and read loads of books regarding network marketing, business and entrepreneurialism and lots of books about personal development and improving communication.

It was a fantastic feeling to get a standing ovation in front of 3000 people for hitting the first milestone called Team Leader (this is known as T.L.). Which means you have personally gathered ten customers and recruited 3 people who have accumulated at least three customers, and between yourself and the team, there are 50 customers altogether.

One of the ways to build a business and contacts was by doing promotional 'Win a Mini' events. These can be set up anywhere, garden fetes, craft fairs, festivals, summer events, B&Qs, Wickes, and The Range etc.

As a distributor, you have to pay for venue hire or space to put up a gazebo or a stall, that can become expensive. Over the years I have bought myself two gazebos as I snapped one of them, which was not even mine, I had borrowed it from a carer. I have also purchased different banners that continuously need updating due to various promotions and tonnes of promotional merchandise.

Me and one of my carers, who was involved in the business, had an outstanding run at Tesco in Gainsborough for a few months. The lady who organised it was very disorganised. We would quite often turn up on an agreed day, only to find another charity or promotion was going on so she would tell us to come back another day and do it for free. We found this happened at least half a dozen times, which was great.

The idea is you want to get people to enter into the free prize draw, and they can win a Mini or £10 000. Once you have entered them in the competition, you tell them a little bit about the services that are available or tell them about the business opportunity depending on what boxes they tick on the questionnaire.

This is a great way to meet people and build your list of potential prospects and arrange appointments to go out and see people, sometimes they are incredibly successful and sometimes they are a complete waste of time. The majority of my U.W. business growth was from 'Win a Mini'.

However, nothing is guaranteed, and sometimes they are hugely unsuccessful, and they can be very tedious and very annoying. Sometimes waiting for people to fill in forms can take a long time. The events can also be weather dependent, and I often found myself sitting out in cold, wet, windy days under a gazebo.
One summer family day out was so bad we played a full game of Monopoly on an iPad until completion as we were unable to get the gazebo off the site but we still managed to get a couple of appointments though.

The best way to make them work was to hand out entry slips at the entrance, so people would come to ask to be entered into the competition. Some of my carers didn't have a problem with it, but some refused to do it, which caused tension between carers and myself and also between other distributors.

Some people would help me throughout the day with basic tasks, which mainly involved picking up the clipboard which kept falling on the floor, writing down addresses and times, helping to give out brochures etc. I always tried to be as independent as possible, but there are somethings I can't do.

Most people were helpful, although I found some were going behind my back and moaning and complaining about me to other people especially my upline, that caused more tension. People would be eager enough to accept a cup of tea or hot chocolate though.

My carers were always nearby to help with care or tasks. Often, they would go for a wander or a bite to eat or for a drink or go to the toilet etc, but they were always only a phone call away, and I never asked anyone to get involved with personal care or giving me a bite to eat.

I often found doing these events was incredibly frustrating. Sometimes people wouldn't make eye contact, as if you could catch being disabled! I lost track of the number of times people were just willing to give me money assuming I was a charity, which was patronising as all I was trying to do was get a bit of extra money to help better my life.

I often felt people were avoiding me just because I use a powerchair. I think a lot of people just said yes to be nice and then the minute they got home they cancelled.

I know cancellations are part of the process, but so many people would arrange an appointment and then not be in or cancel the very minute they got home. It was frustrating when you arrange a meeting to turn up at the allocated time to find no one was home. I even had times where I could see them hiding behind settees, not even willing to answer the door.

Access was always an issue getting into people's homes, but I was still determined to find a way. Sometimes I could get in okay and sometimes I had to use my ramps, and it was very tricky. I often worry about knocking things about in people's homes and not being able to get out. I adapted on many occasions and made the most of what I could. I found this involved doing presentations on drives, in garages, or meeting at local cafes, pubs or libraries. Anywhere where I could sit and talk. I felt this wasn't always practical especially when it was cold.

Most people were accommodating and tried to help get me in their home, but sometimes it just couldn't be done, which caused me no end of stress.

I tried doing letter drops, but this also caused issues trying to avoid scratching cars and damaging plants etc.

I did earn a lot of respect within the network for adapting to situations and continuing to work the business, and it was great to get the recognition when I felt I deserved it by either getting promoted or generally doing well and gathering customers or partners. However, when I was doing rubbish at the business and not enjoying it, I often found when I attended meetings, pieces of training or events, I became a token poster picture for disability.

I know the idea was that if I could do the business with my disability, then anyone could, which is okay. I often have people contacting me to find out how I have overcome some of the issues. However, when it wasn't going well, and motivation was low, and I had no passion for it, it was incredibly frustrating to be dragged in front of large groups of people to tell my story. The worst time was at an event I went to which was run by one of the prominent leaders in the company to help improve my motivation, and without warning he had me speaking in front of 200 people. It felt so forced, and I thought I just had to say the right thing to please everyone else, while I was dying inside. I just wanted to say how I felt about the business, not what people wanted to hear.

I was asked once to do a brief talk on access issues and some of the situations I had overcome, which I was fine with. However, one of the leaders phoned me to do a pre-prep, I was pretty sure this wasn't the person who was going to be interviewing me, and the subject matter was different, which I'm pretty sure I explained.

He asked how many times I went to presentation evenings and training sessions etc. Which I had been to plenty of but according to him it wasn't enough, and he pretty much called me a fraud as I wasn't following the system and toeing the company line as much as expected. Suffice to say I was not impressed with this at all. I have never been a fraud at anything I have done in my entire life. Everything I have done and achieved has been from hard work, effort and from overcoming barriers and situations that I have come across regularly. I did notice I was removed from his WhatsApp group, but then a few months later I was asked to talk at one of his meetings, which I didn't do.

Every three months the company put on a significant event, this enabled you to associate with other members and hear company announcements. I always tried to get to these as they helped to keep me motivated and be inspired by the speakers. I listened to some fantastic speakers giving some great tips. I usually came away from these events buzzing and prepared to keep doing what was necessary to make it successful.

I never liked misleading people and arranging to see people without them knowing what it was about first, as we were taught to do. The reason behind this was that they had no preconception about the services or the business. It was a great way of getting in touch with old friends and having a chat, but when you had an agenda, it never felt natural.

I never liked bugging people and continuously asking and inviting them to meetings, although a lot of people would have benefited, I'm sure. I did get on a lot of people's nerves, and I found I started seeing people just as prospects or potential customers, when they should be friends and if the timing became better or circumstances changed then people would join.

I did make some good friends from doing the business, but it's always tricky and awkward if they are not doing well or not getting involved, especially between friends as it alters the relationship. I tried to help them as much as possible but felt I was annoying them to get involved.

I did expect it to grow financially quicker than it did, and I spent more on promotions, going to events and fuel than I expected.

I found it awkward at social events when I wasn't doing well always trying to be positive when inside I was feeling very cynical about the whole business.

The main thing I liked about the business though is getting paid over and over again for doing a job once. Once a customer has been successfully signed up and, as long as they pay their bill every month, you get a small percentage of their spend, and if people move into the houses as new owners, the chances are they would gain and retain the services so in effect you were hopefully signing up the house as a customer for years to come.

I loved the self-development which I embraced, and I learnt a lot about network marketing, business and being an entrepreneur.

I also loved getting a free pizza and a beer for getting a customer and even better getting 2, 1 for me and 1 for my carer. This is called Pizza Tuesday, and once a month people meet at Pizza Express and can exchange tips, advice and motivate each other.

The biggest downfall and challenge always came down to cost as there are still offers and deals from the major competition and they were not always the cheapest. People didn't see the value in awards and fantastic customer services or free L.E.Ds fitted and repaired or discounted shopping and dining costs.

Over the years I must have handed out numerous flyers, business cards, letters, and brochures. I have no idea how many, but my number would have been given to people, I would guess into the thousands. I got called and asked for information or an appointment maybe five times.

Picking up the phone became a real burden and a chore and a confidence crusher. I had to motivate myself to pick up the phone even if it had been arranged, which annoyed me, as the one thing I can do is talk. I can talk about my life and injury to strangers but making a phone call just felt awkward and alien and sales oriented at times, which isn't me at all.

The compensation plan had its flaws. Once you got over 20 customers, you did get paid on your customer's telephony however you needed 50 customers to get paid on the electric and gas unless you gathered a customer every month. Which I felt demoralising when I knew I had tried my hardest but had not managed to get a customer. I got penalised for this even though the customer was still paying their bill and the company was still getting their money.

Most people do U.W. for time freedom or money freedom. I have the time and do okay for money to get by, but I struggle when I am hit with big bills or unexpected ones or trying to save for expensive items or holidays. I had to redecorate my house on my credit card and needed a bit more. I find it hard to justify giving my free time for events, promotional events and using the little money I have to cover the costs of trying to build a U.W. business!

I did find it counter-productive though and having to deal with all the issues got me down and crushed my confidence and became soul destroying!
There are better ways I found to do presentations and I may pick it back up in the future but at the end of the day my heart was not in it, and it did not make me happy.

Getting to team leader and getting a standing ovation
was a great feeling

21
KLIFE

After the summer of 2015, I wanted to look for something different to do to get some money in over the Christmas period, and I came across the Klife catalogue, which was part of Kleeneze and there were a lot of good gift ideas in there.

Somehow, I found out about the business behind it as people were selling on Facebook. It seemed appealing to me as you could advertise for free, I thought I might as well join as a partner and get the commission back on the Christmas presents, I would be buying anyway.

I got some catalogues as part of signing up to become a distributor, and I posted some out to neighbours, friends, and family and sold quite a few items.

We had a new promotion on at the time from Utility Warehouse about getting free L.E.Ds so I thought it would be a good idea to post lots of brochures offering the products and a leaflet about Utility Warehouse as well, but I only had a few people show interest.

I joined lots of groups on Facebook and sold quite a lot leading up to Christmas. It was straightforward to post into local selling groups, but you had to do it a lot and get lots of catalogues out at the same time. I liked the idea of building a team and getting a small percentage of what they earned, and I liked the idea of being able to buy quality leads, as I am not good at recruiting, although they didn't turn out to be quality. Every Tom Dick and Harry responded to the advertisements that the company put out looking for people to earn an extra income.

I don't like the idea of once you had someone interested in the business you hand them control and just send them to a website, when they say they are going to sign up, and they don't. I prefer having control over these things to make sure it's correct.

The way the company worked was okay in the sense that you ordered the products and then you got invoiced, and it was up to you to get the product out, sometimes it was easy, and people came to my house, this worked out well as I was also able to introduce them to U.W. There were times that people wanted products and it turned out they never answered the phone or weren't in when you went to deliver. I also found it difficult monitoring profit as you got paid cash off people and I had already paid the invoice.

185

I did it for a few months and then didn't bother with it anymore. I never really got going with this business and never saw it as a long-term venture. I didn't start building a team and didn't put much effort in. A couple of years later the whole of Kleeneze went into liquidation. I was glad I did not give it much effort!

22

4 NETWORKING

I joined the 4N networking group towards the end of 2017, with an open mind. I was hoping to get myself out there more to promote my books and to do talks to create awareness about living with a spinal injury and living with any disability. Having decided not to support U.W. for a while and realising that my biggest asset was my experiences and myself and that I should be more focused on what I can offer myself.

Networking is an excellent way of meeting people, and you never know who you are going to interact with. I aimed to meet people who can help me with proofreading, editing, marketing, etc. I wanted to meet people who can help me with more tips and get good advice on motivational speaking and find places where I can get in front of people.

Each meeting is broken down to having a meal where everyone introduces themselves and what they do in 40 seconds, which is an excellent way of improving your quick pitch and making it more concise. Then arranging to have three separate 10 minutes one-on-one chats with various people from different backgrounds and businesses.

Some can be very interesting and helpful and have been able to point me in the right direction or help with contacts. With some it is evident that it's not going to be beneficial to either person, and sometimes it's good to sell and sign a book or 2.

After each set of individual meetings, there is a four sight, which is a 20-minute talk or demonstration, which is an insight into a specialist subject or interest. It is not meant to be a sales pitch. Some are fascinating and well told, and some are not. 4N has been hugely beneficial to me as it gave me a safe place to practice my talks, and I was able to pick out which bits are the most powerful and have the most impact. Due to the size of the meetings being around 20, I was able to build my confidence in my own story, and myself. 4N was a great place to improve and practice speaking in public and a great way to improve my knowledge.

Getting involved in the network was a great decision as it has opened up many doors. Some people's services and businesses are not helpful to my requirements. Over a few months, I have found people I can work with who have pointed me in the right direction, including a proofreader and publisher, website developer, someone to make a promotional video and somebody to help me with marketing.

I did feel the meetings were beneficial at times and I got a lot out of them. The quarterly subscription was expensive for me, as I had to pay £15 for each meal at each meeting. I was hoping it would open up more avenues for me but it did not. I decided to have a break from it and maybe revisit it in the future.

23
CASHING IN ON CRYPTOCURRENCIES

I have had a few ups and downs trying to make a few extra quid online. A friend told me about a new cryptocurrency which could be worth investing in before they hit the market, these are called I.C.Os or Initial Coin Offerings. I spent $47 on 50 of these particular coins called Regal Coins.

It was a nightmare trying to buy them in the first place, the company was only allowing a handful to be purchased at specific times, and due to different time zones, there was no way of knowing what the best time would be to buy. They were selling out extremely quickly. Usually, I would have tried 2 or 3 times and given up, thinking it was only $47 so it was not worth the hassle. There wasn't much hype, and I was going by who had mentioned it to me. I tried at different times in the day on numerous occasions for at least a week! Others I knew who were trying to get them just gave up. I don't know why I kept trying, but eventually, I got my 50 coins showing up in my account.

When they went on the exchange in the first week, they went straight in at about $20 or $30 each, so I was very excited. Within the first week, they went to about $50 each. I decided to sell half of mine, which meant I banked £550, which paid off a good chunk of my credit card. I was a bit panicky for a few weeks after, as there wasn't much communication from the company and every time, I logged in to the site it was just showing maintenance, and they were changing servers.

I saw that people's accounts were slowly getting unlocked, I panicked a bit, but the price was still high. I converted them to Bitcoin as soon as I could and managed to bank another £1300! With this, I paid off another £500 of my credit card that had accumulated over the summer while I was redecorating my house.

Getting £1800 on a return for a $47 investment blew me away, I had no idea this would be the outcome! I needed to pay off my credit card, which I did immediately. However, I didn't quite realise at the time what the Bitcoin market was going to do and once I had paid off my debts and reinvested elsewhere the price of Bitcoin skyrocketed within the next two months. I had 0.3 of a Bitcoin, and the price went up to £15000 per coin. If only I had held off selling and hung onto it and sold at the highest point, which would have been tricky as once the price kept going up, there would have been no reason to sell. Potentially I could have turned $47 into £5000. The rate dropped a lot in 2018, so it could have lost value. Hindsight is a beautiful thing, if only there had been a crystal ball. A few months later I was curious about the price, and when I checked, they were worth a pittance.

I was able to get out of debt and invest some for my future into different currencies. This investment indeed turned out to be a game changer and what I reinvested is going to make a massive difference to my life. Sometimes in life things go perfectly and work out for the best, sometimes they don't!

24
HOW NOT TO MAKE MONEY

A couple of years ago I decided to look to the Internet to see if I could make a few quid. I have always heard of people making money off the Internet, but I never knew where to start or what to trust.

I came across an opportunity called Traffic Monsoon from someone I met from strange circumstances and coincidences. As I keep saying, I am a big believer in things happening for a reason, and meeting people when the time is right.

While out doing a letter drop for U.W. one day. We took it in turns to knock on the door. Adam who was a carer at the time happened to get an appointment that converted to a good customer about 15 metres from my home, which was annoying, but it was one of those things. There were a couple of technical issues setting up their broadband, and he had to keep popping round, the customer's husband kept going on about this opportunity and how well he was doing. I was unaware of this, but I came across this opportunity from 2 or 3 people online. I mentioned it to Adam who told me this other chap did it. I felt it beneficial if I would join under him as he was local and I could get advice and guidance, he was also one of the people who promoted it to others at presentation evenings.

The company offered online advertising that was something I knew nothing about, but I guessed there would be a lot of money in advertising online and the opportunity sounded good. You purchased advertising packs for $50 and over a period got $55 back; meaning if you compounded earnings, it was apparent that over time a lot of money could be made. This sounded great, and lots of people were making lots of money from it. I bought one pack first, and I could see it was working so I decided to put some money in which brought me some advertising so, I could promote other things.

After a couple of months, there were issues with PayPal, and they stopped and held all the customer's money, which caused problems and created red flags with a governing body that froze all the accounts and eventually took the company to court for being a fraudulent Ponzi scheme. The owner argued against this due to the fact that they were selling advertising. It did go through the courts, and a conclusion was never actually given to the members. All accounts were frozen, and thousands of people lost thousands of pounds.

I got to know a few people from this company all around the world and as new opportunities came along. I was often asked to look at promotional videos and webinars. Most of which I turned down because I had been burnt.

I did join a few though and could see people doing well with them. Frankly, the good thing about not having much money is I don't invest much. Therefore, I can't lose much, but people do put thousands into these systems promising high returns. I got addicted to the chase and the fun of it but lost out too many times.

I joined some that lasted a couple of weeks and then crashed. I joined one called Gladiacoin that promised to double your Bitcoin in 90 days or less, and at the time I thought I had entered an outstanding team. People were being put in my group left, right and centre, and it started growing well really quickly, and a lot of people were making a lot of money. I could see the results that other people were getting, and I could look at my results growing and thought I had found a goldmine. I did not withdraw any earnings but kept letting it compound and then all of a sudden, I couldn't even log in to the website and just like that it was gone with everyone's money.

I joined another one, which promised a high daily return, and within weeks there was no ability to withdraw your funds. I kept checking this website, and I could see the compound interest was still going up, but there was no way of getting the money out. These scammers must have made a fortune out of this as people put their money in and a company or person was still getting the compounded interest, but no one was able to withdraw, and even a few months later somehow the website was still up, but there was no way of getting any money out.

I tried to avoid these dodgy scams but have a tendency of making stupid drunken decisions late at night and then waking up in the morning seeing an email saying I had joined something new.

One that I joined wanted a monthly subscription and offered a free trial period of some software. I found I didn't want the software anyway so put in a support ticket to cancel my subscription during the trial period to which I got no response. I put another support ticket in and had no answer from that either. There was no direct debit set up, but yet they still managed to keep taking my money, I contacted my bank and reported my card lost, so they cancelled it, and I got my money back from the bank. However, the so-called company challenged the fact and said I hadn't tried to cancel the subscription and I hadn't put a support ticket and so they ended up taking the money back off me.

I went through the same thing with USI-TECH, after lots of research and talks with other members, I joined. I heard about these quite early and decided against it. I had kept an eye on the company, and it seemed like they were going to be a massive player in the cryptocurrency industry. They were investing millions into mining farms, cryptocurrency ATMs, revolutionary new technology to minimise electricity costs and their coins. Their cryptocurrency never even got off the ground, and a lot of people lost a lot of money. They stopped paying and seemed to disappear promising to pay everyone back, but I was not holding my breath! I did manage to withdraw some earnings when I started seeing red flags.

I.C.O. stands for an Initial Coin Offering and the idea is that coins or tokens are sold at a meagre price to the public in limited supply before they are submitted to any exchange, which usually means that the initial investment made by the company goes towards the development and creation of the token, sometimes known as crowdfunding. Most companies release what is called a white paper, which is a path the company intends to take to make the coin available and hopefully successful.

The first one I got involved in is called Electroneum. I got involved in this as a lot of people were talking about it and it was very cheap at $0.01 per coin, I felt it was worth a gamble. The thing that interested me about this was the fact they are trying to bring cryptocurrency more commercially available to mobile users, and this particular coin is going to be focused around mobile phones and gambling apps, both of which are huge industries. I invested about £50 into this project, and by referring others; I ended up with 4700 tokens. At one point mine were worth 500 quid, but I did not sell. After the first year a lot is going on in the project but at the time of writing the coins had little value.

I bought a few Dascoin and Token Pay mainly because of the hype and those who had suggested them to me. The projects may take off, but at the moment they have a little amount of dollar value!

Token Pay coins were a hassle from the very beginning, and I bought them as a recommendation. It showed up on my back office for them, that I had purchased them, but they never turned up. I put four or five support tickets in and never got a response.

After about three or four months I gave up on them and felt as though I had been ripped off. I eventually got a message from the support team saying they would look into my case, and that I had to find the original transaction details of the purchase. All transactions via Bitcoin can be traced when you know what you're doing. I saw all the pertinent information and bounced backwards and forwards with the support team for weeks.

I had no end to problems getting a wallet secure on my PC. I think I created problems for myself by downloading another wallet that overrode the first one, therefore, creating a new wallet address. It took weeks to finally sort this out and get the tokens that I had paid for. I had purchased 60 tokens for around £100 and somehow ended up with 54. They said it was due to fees, even though they would have been paid when I initially bought the tokens. I read a lot of hype about these being the next big thing.
I felt when they got to $5 each it was a good time to get rid of them. I made about £80 and got my seed money back and was happy with that, so these were not a total loss. If the coins do become the next big thing and are worth a lot of money in 12 or 24 months, then it's just one of those things.

I have been involved in a few Rev Shares, Matrices, High Yield investment programmes that have amounted to nothing but loss and frustration.

I felt quite embarrassed writing this, falling for the same crap in different disguises but it's part of life's learning curve and mistakes, and it helps strengthen your character and hopefully something to learn from. It gives you a better idea of what to look out for. Is there a genuine product behind the business? Is there an actual owner? Is that owner transparent and open? Do they seem real? Is the business built for long-term sustainability? Or is it just another scam?

Just like everything else in life sometimes you have to sort out the rubbish before you come across the gems!

25
HOPE ONLINE

Bitcoin started at a ridiculously low price in 2009. You could buy them for pence, and quite a few people did and made a fortune from this. There are tons of stories about people getting involved and selling them ridiculously low and not hanging on and seeing the potential of this revolutionary new technology and way of using money online in a completely decentralised manner.

I started hearing about it in around 2015 when one of my best mates was interested and involved in trading it. At the time you could get one for about £300. I didn't have a clue what he was talking about–block chains, private keys and hash rates blah de blah!

More people I was speaking to online were getting involved in the whole industry, and when one Bitcoin became about £1 000, I started taking an interest, so far, the highest value Bitcoin was £15 000 in December 2017!

I believe it will go above this and beyond at some point! There is no way I am missing the second chance of it reaching an all-time high. All the other coins seem to increase or decrease in value due to

Bitcoin. At the start of 2019, the whole market was at a low and showed no signs of recovery. Who knows what the cost will be in the future!

The principal hopes I have online are from 2 companies I am involved in, which are both cryptocurrency-based. One is called Powerhouse Network, and the other is Zukul. I had got to know the owners of Powerhouse Network online from doing webinars and hangouts showing how to use social media for promoting while they were in Zukul. They then created their own company that I followed but did not get involved in at the start. The owners are 100% transparent, both from the U.K. and are ex-forces, both are disciplined, driven and focused with a keen interest in helping others, and they have got some fantastic programmers and traders on board.

Initially, I got involved because they had a passive income earning system from cryptocurrency mining, but they were leasing equipment. The company started planning its infrastructure to be self-sustainable, by creating their mining facility, which is in Croatia, creating their exchange and having their programming team available. They expected to have various cryptocurrencies. The mining farm and the first coin they released as an I.C.O. is called Polaris, these are ERC20 tokens and use the Ethereum blockchain not the Bitcoin one. I bought some of these with my profits from Regal Coin. They started working on different charitable coins, which are in the early stages at the moment.

There are projects to help refugees affected by war, veterans affected by conflicts, assisting children with disabilities in Canada get involved with sports especially winter ones, people who have suffered strokes and heart conditions and a project to help children less fortunate than others in Croatia.

I used profits from Regal Coin to buy Polaris, which is the main asset. I initially bought some at $0.20. I won a few by helping share the company online and when their exchange went live. People were selling at ridiculously low prices. I bought lots of them. People don't see the vision that I see and are willing to settle for short-term gratification instead of long-term reward!

I did not join them all but got in early with 3 of the projects when coins were $0.01 each and as the currency went through stages of the I.C.O. The price increased.

I didn't spend much, but I bought a few thousand of each. Even if the coins are not successful then at least I know I have helped out the causes above. I plan to hang onto most of mine and see what happens. Short-term gain is still significant to me to get seed money back. However, I am leaving them for the long term. The company is going to be self-sufficient and have created their decentralised exchange and created their blockchain using the best of Bitcoin technology and the best of Ethereum. The initial tokens created have been changed to an original cryptocurrency called Eureka and are going to be available on more significant exchanges.

They have a buyback and burn strategy which means when everything comes together with the exchange, and the mining and trading are more in effect. The more transactions created on the blockchain, the more coins are burnt out of circulation which decreases supply and increases demand as there will only be a certain number in circulation. Profits from other projects under the same umbrella such as mining and trading will continuously and slowly increase the buyback and burn strategy. The company has just released their own social media platform and have partnered up with real estate and car selling sites, which means advertising and exposure.

There is a ton of work to be done on each project, and hopefully, they will all become successful, so hopefully this time next year ....

Zukul has been by far the most prominent online roller coaster. I joined this in 2015. Zukul is an online marketing suite that offers all essential tools to work online such as a landing page creator, which is a capture page, so when someone sees your offer, they put their email in and get added to your list, then they receive email sequences to make them join an opportunity or hopefully buy a product. They offer to host for blogs, a URL shortening tool and a banner creator, which is a flashing, banner that advertises your opportunity or product. These can be linked to websites or rev-shares where people are surfing ads online or used to buy traffic or visitors to your site. For a few dollars, you pay for the amount of people that click the banner.

They had an excellent commission plan, as the company is a Multi-Level Marketing network business. A lot of people made money from this, and I made some! It was based on a monthly subscription that I paid for a long time but lost faith in it and downgraded so I could keep using the marketing tools, which are great value, easy-to-use and loads of training available and I was able to hold my position in the company.

An advertising platform was created where you could advertise on the web and also buy ad packs for different prices and while people were clicking ten ads a day, showing other people's offers you earned from the profits generated by the advertising. The system worked a treat for six months, but I never withdrew any profits and kept putting it back into compound earnings. It started slowing down, and people were not earning. The owner seemed very determined not to let them fail and tried a few solutions, one of which was a 'done for you' marketing system, which had some excellent training and places to either buy or advertise for free, using the available tools.

As Bitcoin grew and grew, the owner was doing more trading and said he was working on an automated trading robot. He showed us how to read exchanges and how to trade Bitcoin for Fiat currency, but it was extremely time consuming, and complicated and difficult to judge if the price would go up or down. After nine months of development and working with his programming team, by March 2018 it was nearly ready for testing, and as a loyal customer, I was able to get in on the testing stage.

The first thing I like about it is the simplicity, and the best thing is the company does not hold the money. It stays on an exchange which is owned by the world's biggest cryptocurrency wallet which is exceptionally secure, and at any point, I could either hold cryptocurrency or Fiat currency and can get access to both, but obviously if Bitcoin doesn't reach its target price, it could lose value. It buys low and sells at a profit. Trading can be done manually, and it is not giving financial advice, it takes the emotion and decision-making out of the process so is entirely legit. There is a monthly subscription, which is split and pays people above as in any M.L.M. I paid for my first month and the next month was paid for by the original compensation plan developed years before so my bot would be free to use as long as people keep using the tool.

It can trade Bitcoin, Bitcoin Cash, Ethereum or Lite coin with Pound Sterling, Euros or Dollars.
A minimum return of investment is set, and the bot will not sell below that price. I have been averaging between 2% to 4 %, and the highest I have seen was a return of 12.5%. The robots work a treat when price increases but not so much in a down market.

The company started developing a binary trading robot, which can trade any stock or commodity on the market. The basic concept is betting whether the prices paired will rise or fall in the next minute on autopilot. I could not justify the cost to use the software, and it will be interesting to see what happens.

It's been a long journey, but no one said trying to create passive incomes and build a better life, and financial security for myself, instead of being in the system on benefits, would be an easy one. From tiny seeds, oak trees are born, but to reap the rewards, you have to sow the seeds first!

26
PUBLIC SPEAKING

Public speaking is something I am looking at doing more. I hope to be able to get into schools and tell my story to younger people, with the hope of educating and showing them that disabilities should not be ignored, and people with disabilities are just people who may need a bit of assistance or help, but they can live good healthy lives, and achieve amazing things. I would also like to do more at networking and business events as I really like the entrepreneurs mindset. Spinal hospitals would be good to.

I don't tend to talk about my life and my injury to large groups of people. I had previously spoken for about 10 or 15 minutes about the S.A.N.D. sports club for the Women's Institute and a charity called Inner Wheel as they had raised money for the club.

Talking about the S.A.N.D. sports club isn't a problem as it is an excellent club for children with disabilities and something I enjoy and am passionate about. I have been asked to speak at numerous C.O.Ps for Utility Warehouse, but all that involves is, saying your name, and your background and where you live.

I have also done various PowerPoint presentations throughout college and university about multiple subjects that usually had lasted about 10 minutes, which were in a safe environment with people I knew.

I joined a business networking group called 4N, having come to the conclusion that I had been a bit lost and confused about where and what direction I was heading. I wanted to be more active in promoting my books, my story and myself.

I had met Tony Leakes previously who represents a company/business called Positive Changes. I knew he was a confident guy and a public speaker. I knew he did life coaching and mentoring and was involved in Neuro-Linguistic Programming. I was very interested to know more about what he did, and during the breakfast meeting, I wanted to have a 10-minute one-on-one with him to see if we could work together or if I could get some pointers.

We chatted briefly and arranged to have a proper one-to-one at my house. We both thought there could be synergy between how I live my life and the theory that he spoke. We got on well, and we chatted about potentially turning my injury and recovery into a motivational speech, and what I would like to get out of it and why I wanted to get involved in public speaking.

It turned out in a couple of weeks he had been asked to do a talk on limitations and overcoming them as part of a graduation ceremony for a human resources business at Yorkshire Wildlife Park. He offered me the opportunity to split the session with him and do 10 minutes each. I thought it sounded like a great idea.

As I have mentioned before, I often find when the timing is right opportunities present themselves, and things seem to fall into place quickly, and all coincidences become synchronised as though the universe is saying this is the right direction to go in and everything is pulled together to work.

I feel that a picture says a thousand words and I have some great photos of what I have done and things I have achieved over the years. I did not have very long, but I wanted to show a few of my favourite pictures. I got some slides together to help tell my story. I find it is a lot easier when I have images behind me as it is a visual representation and I do not have to explain what the equipment looks like and how it works. For example, the ski cart is quite a difficult thing to explain and can take a few minutes, where a simple picture says it all.

Tony sent me a recording of what he was going to say, and I was very impressed and quite worried that I wouldn't be entirely up to his standard as he has been speaking publicly for a while. I did a quick run through to get a measure of time, and I was at about 8 minutes. I'm not a read from the script kind of guy, and my preparation was in creating the PowerPoint presentation. I feel it's better to speak from the heart as long as you know the bullet points.

When we turned up on the day, the marquee was set out to look very posh, and everyone was in their caps and gowns, and all the family and friends were there to join in the celebration. I think there were about 200 people there in total.

It was fascinating hearing the CEO talk about how he grew and developed Yorkshire Wildlife Park, initially, I felt a little bit nervous about talking about overcoming limitations at such a prestigious event, the idea was from their point of view to help people move forward once they had got the qualification.

The first few minutes I was terrified. I had so many things going through my head. How do I start? Will I choke? Is my voice going to hold? Will I speak clearly? Will I forget the critical points? Am I going to be any good? How many people are going to be listening? Will they ask questions? Will they laugh at my jokes? Will I get my message across? Are they going to hear? What's my name? Who am I? What am I doing? Why did I say yes to this? And breathe...

I agreed with Tony that he would turn the slides of my PowerPoint presentation, but once I got started, I forgot to tell him to change the slides, so I was a little bit out of sync with what I was saying and what was on the screen. I realised this about halfway through, and I told him to turn the slides as required. Afterwards, my carer told me she had recognised this and was nodding and saying to him turn the slides. I set my alarm for 10 minutes, and it went quick. I was only about halfway through my presentation when I heard the signal going off. I panicked here because I didn't know how to stop the alarm from beeping. Luckily it went off quite quickly, so I had to fly through it.

People were engaged and listened to some of the barriers and limitations I have overcome from dealing with my injury and adapting to life as a wheelchair user and living independently, to going skiing and learning to sail on my own, and some of the challenges faced while travelling to Egypt and doing a safari. It worked well with Tony's section after mine.

My practical way of overcoming limits and having to deal with different obstacles and his knowledge of the subject from a psychological viewpoint worked well together. Thankfully he recorded this and when I heard it back days later, I was delighted with the results and it sounded excellent, although extraordinarily rushed and I spoke practically not emotionally. I received some excellent feedback, and it was an honour to speak at a graduation ceremony!

The next talk I did was in a kebab shop with five people. 1 being my carer and 1 being a mate. It was an excellent chance to try out my projector that my dad got me for Christmas, which was arranged from a 4N meeting not just at random. I thought there would be more people there and couldn't be bothered to go into any depth, detail or emotion. I asked at the start what would happen if my meal turned up, I was told to carry on and have my dinner while talking, I need feeding so would have just left the food.

I felt I did okay but got some harsh feedback, and I was told there was not enough emotion. Not enough time spent talking about my injury (for me it was so long ago, and I accept it, and I am quite blasé about it) and not enough drama. I got told that I was too casual. It was a potentially compelling story. I did get a free meal though, which was horrible. I was quite glad afterwards that I put no effort in as I learnt that no matter how small the audience; you don't know what kind of input they give, and the feedback made me up my game.

I went back through my notes from initially talking to Tony on how we could develop and get the strongest impact out of my story and had to make some drastic changes to make it more powerful quickly. I am very thankful I got to spend some time working with him and got to hear him first hand. I felt I learnt a lot from him and thought he helped me understand the best out of my story.

The next morning, I was due to do my first 20 minutes 4 sight for 4N, so I amped it up and started with a powerful statement of how I felt on the day and went for full impact and went through every emotion and every challenge. I pushed myself to the point of feeling and reliving everything I had been through and dealt with within the time constraints and I didn't hold back.

I talked about how I felt at the beginning when I first found out about the severity of the break! How it felt to see an x-ray of my broken neck! How it felt having three months flat on my back after my skull had been drilled into, to have weights hanging from my head

215

unable to move my head or any part of my body! What it was like being in a hospital for eight months! How there was very little physiotherapy I could do, other than having my muscles stretched daily! How it felt seeing other people transferring themselves into wheelchairs, knowing I would never be able to do it, as I need hoisting for transferring! I talked about seeing people staying at the halfway house next to the hospital knowing I would be shoved in a nursing home! I talked about how I had to learn to drive a powerchair left-handed even though before my injury I was right-handed. My left-hand sensation and movements came back first, and I kept getting stuck in lifts, corners and flowerbeds!

I talked about going skiing for the first time in Sweden and how I had no idea how to travel in a wheelchair! I spoke of the excitement, freedom, independence, hope and optimism I felt from being able to ski again! I talked about the freedom I experienced and the feeling of achievement being ready to sail solo, and what it felt like to nearly capsize! I spoke about living independently and moving into my own home! I talked about going to Egypt and how many obstacles and barriers I came across to see the great pyramids with my dad! I talked about how many obstacles and barriers I overcame to see a hippo at the bottom of a valley in South Africa!

216

I talked about how I enrolled in a physical sports coaching course with a physical disability! I spoke of the moment I rolled across the stage for my graduation and claimed my Bachelor of Arts degree! I talked about writing my first book, Life Rolls On!

I had the group listening and feeling every emotion and step of my journey and got them asking themselves how they would have handled such trauma.

I got told it was one of the most potent 4 sights some of the people had heard and I went on and delivered a similar talk 5 or 6 times. I felt it was the first time I changed from being a public speaker into a motivational speaker!

At one of the 4N networking meetings, there was someone who studied psychology and was setting up his networking group based more on positivity, and he asked me to speak at his networking event as he was very impressed with me, I even made him cry with my talk.

Square Peg it's called as everyone is different and square pegs don't fit in round holes, and the idea is to make a fit and celebrate people's individuality, and uniqueness and all come together. The first event was more sales orientated and had some fantastic speakers, so I was asked to speak at the next one and the theme became authenticity and resilience.

Timing was a bit more relaxed, and the atmosphere was great with about 75 people. I was able to expand my story more and focus on the resilience of the human spirit aspect. I did about 30 minutes and 10 minutes Q&A and was looking and gauging the reactions of the audience and could see they were taken on an emotional roller coaster. I felt I pulled everything together and did my best talk yet!

I have been asked to speak for a few external events from doing this ranging from schools, Cubs and Brownies, a more massive networking event and the Fibromyalgia Society. I feel this is the direction I want to be putting my time and energy into, so time will tell where it leads me. This time next year...

27
MOTIVATION

One thing I am always asked is what motivates me
and what keeps me going. One of the main things that
drives me is personal development. I am continually
growing as a person, without any personal growth
how do you know where you are going? There have
been mistakes on the way, but this is also how we
learn and grow.

I see challenges and obstacles as a way of personal
growth. Every time I challenge myself, and every time
I push myself a little bit harder, it is taking me more
and more away from my disability, more towards self-
actualisation, building self-esteem and creating some
normality. Every task or adventure is always a little
bit harder and puts me more out of my comfort zone.

I love adventure and trying different things and seeing
different places especially doing physical activities. I
like to push myself and prove to myself that the
disability does not matter and to show people and
myself what can be achieved.

I never really cared for school and education when I
was younger. Since my injury, I have gained lots of
sports qualifications and my degree. I love reading or

listening to audiobooks to keep learning and educating myself on various subjects.

I do get a lot of satisfaction from helping others whether it is in a coaching environment or from my talks or books especially with regards to breaking down barriers for disability.

One of my main driving factors is to be more financially stable, not for the money itself but for what can be done with it. Things like powerchairs and vehicles cost a lot of money, and I would rather be self-sufficient and be able to afford these things especially when they break or need fixing.

I would also like to be able to travel more. My dad has been great with money, and I would not have been able to have such a good quality of life without his help, but I would much rather be able to afford things on my own.

I do have a lot of time on my hands, and sometimes it is challenging to fill the time. Sometimes I'm quite happy staying at home watching TV, playing games etc. I need constant stimulation and challenges which is why I am always looking for something different to do or try.

I did an online questionnaire once by the great Tony Robbins on motivating factors, and the answer it came up with was, uncertainty as a driving factor, which made quite a lot of sense to me as I do like trying different things. I do tend to be very impulsive and jump into things without doing much research. I guess it is the adventure, the excitement and the not quite knowing what will happen. I also find that I get bored quite quickly and once I have achieved something, I like to move on to something different. I usually do find however, that once I set myself a goal, I love to see things through to completion.

The biggest thing for me with regards to motivation is never to let this extremely traumatic thing that happened to me ruin my life. I decided in the hospital to be the best person I can be and make the most of a bad situation, and I never wanted to be a disabled person not contributing to society or having any quality of life so, for me the main thing is just trying to be the best I can be.

The primary motivating factor for me is finding and making sense of this whole situation and finding a purpose and finding a role. I feel that things happen for a reason, but sometimes it takes me a long time and a lot of different stepping stones to find out what the reason may be.

28
F.E.A.R.

Facing fear is an excellent way of improving self-esteem, confidence and helping with personal development. As a person with minimal movement, this is something I come across and have to overcome all the time. F.E.A.R is Face Everything And Rise.

Most of the time I am putting my life in someone else's hands. From the little things like being washed, dressed and transferred from my wheelchair to my bed and vice versa, rolled on the bed for dressing without being dropped, to relying on someone else for driving.

A lot of the time, it is like taking a leap of faith and putting your complete trust in another person or on equipment. Sometimes it is tough to do when people are not feeling one hundred per cent, or you are relying on new people or people you do not know.

Sometimes it is worrying when I am being raised out of a wheelchair over drops of water or being lifted into aeroplane seats. Having people physically lifting the wheelchair especially when I'm in my manual chair, as people tend to lift by the arms and leg rest that click in place.

I do find it difficult to contain my nerves sometimes, and there's quite often an element of doubt. I often feel the anxiety building up, and I have had to learn to control the emotion. In the very early days of my recovery, I used to get so worked up and felt so anxious to the point that I was sometimes sick. I found this was often the case even just going out for a meal or into town. I always feel nervous before doing a talk or presentation, and for a few moments when people are just looking at me before I speak, it can be extremely nerve racking!

I have certainly had many times where I do wonder what I am doing, whether it be getting onto a jeep for a safari, getting into sailing boats, or being prepared to go down a zip wire. Without having these experiences and overcoming the doubts in the first place, then I would have missed out on a lot of different experiences.

Often when I do activities, I put myself forward to go first. The more I sit and wait, the more anxious I get. Sometimes it is best to lead by example and do the activity first, and then other people can see that is safe and I can talk them through the situation, which is the case regarding anything to do with the S.A.N.D. sports club.

I had to learn not to take it personally when people kept saying no to have a new business opportunity, or to save money or to refusing even to enter the prize draw. I just had to keep moving forward. There was a great deal of fear about approaching people and explaining Utility Warehouse. It was crucial to keep learning new skills.

One of the worst things for me is when I am travelling in different vehicles or different countries, and the chair isn't clamped down. It is quite terrifying when the chair starts sliding around. I always know it's not going to go over, but when it is out of my control, it is worrying.
The worst time was in Norway when it was snowy, and we got on a bus, and the chair was sliding everywhere. Not being able to put your arms out or grab onto anything for security can be quite unsettling.

If I had given in at the first hurdle of any activity or been hindered by the fear, then I would have missed out on so many things.

Another fear I had to overcome was people not accepting me for who I am and not being able to get past the wheelchair itself, and it still amazes me how many people see the wheelchair first and not the person. It took me a long time to overcome this, and I just had to rise above the negativity and prove I was the best person I could be.

Having a physical disability and trying to do and achieve different things can be scary and there is 'no one solution fits all' to situations, so I have to weigh up the case and look at different outcomes and find the best way of adapting to get the best possible result, by rising and overcoming any fears.

29
MINDSET OVER MATTER

Having a positive mental attitude is the key to anything in this life, and it has been a long journey for myself to maintain a Positive Mental Attitude. When I first had my injury, I thought and felt that everything I lived for and loved had gone. Initially, I had to go through a grieving process for my old self concept, and at the start, I had no idea how I would cope with such an injury and what my life would be like!

I still look back and wonder how I got through the early days. Family and friends were critical at this time, but I knew I had to try and maintain some positivity in my mind which was difficult while lying motionless with a million thoughts going through my head, which felt like it was in a vice!
Somehow, I was able to get through this challenging stage and through the first year. The main thing that gave me focus and hope was booking into my first skiing holiday with Back Up, which gave me something to focus on although, I had a ton of questions (see Life Rolls On).

Once I had been skiing, I felt I had been given my life back. For the first time, I was able to feel hope and positivity, and I knew I might be able to do other

things and turn my life around after surviving my
accident and getting through year 1.

I eventually moved home. I was only young and knew
I needed something to focus on. I enrolled in college
to start studying sports coaching. I was never a fan of
school. There were better things to do like
skateboarding, boozing and women.

Having lost most of my mobility and having wrecked
my physical body, I knew I had to re-educate myself
and learn how to adapt and manage, and my mind was
my biggest asset. Because I couldn't physically write
notes, I had to focus and concentrate to remember
facts and details. I felt glad to be alive and knew I had
to find purpose and make sense of everything.

I started to develop a 'can do' attitude and approach to
everything and have made a conscious decision never
to quit and never be beaten by my injury. Initially, this
was hard to implement, and I wasn't fully aware and
open to my inner strength. I try to give everything
100% and entirely focus on what I am doing.

Studying counselling was one of the best decisions I
made. I began to understand my unconscious mind
and how hanging onto the physical activities and
adapting to new situations helped me keep my sense

of my identity through all losses of self. I learnt about past experiences, patterns and driving motivating forces.

I learnt about Maslow's hierarchy of needs, which is an excellent way of understanding basic human needs to grow as a person. At the bottom of the pyramid are basic physiological needs such as breathing, food, water, sleep, clothing and shelter. I had started living independently, so these were covered.

Next is safety and security such as health, employment, property, family and social stability. I knew my health was good and had no significant issues after the injury other than paralysis. Work was never going to be a full-time thing, but I started volunteering at the S.A.N.D. club and doing things for college within sports, and I had financial security. Friends and family began to accept me, as still being me and I have some fantastic friends who have helped me through thick and thin, and carers became part of life, and so I made my bungalow my own.

Love and belonging are next, such as friendship, family, intimacy and a sense of connection. By developing closer relationships with friends and family, carers and colleagues, I was able to feel more accepted and more human and finding purpose within the S.A.N.D. club, college, university and businesses.

I have been able to improve self-esteem and build confidence. Achieve the impossible, have respect for others especially people with disabilities. Having counselling myself helped me understand all the processes I had been through such as P.T.S.D. depression, overcoming adversity, understanding concepts of self, grief and loss. These all helped me maintain my independence, my individuality and my identity, which has helped me on numerous occasions achieve self-actualisation! Which is understanding morality, creativity and spontaneity. Being self-aware and accepting yourself, your purpose and inner potential. For me, self-actualisation is vital to be the best person you can be. Going through counselling also helped me develop more resilience and inner strength and helped me understand some of the psychological processes I had been through.

For me, the real way of developing grit, determination, focus, inner strength, willpower and sheer determination is by continually pushing yourself and setting goals. Some of which at the time seems ridiculous but by constantly pushing my limits, boundaries and challenging my perceptions of what I believe to be doable or achievable. Then nothing becomes impossible, and I am only limited by the restrictions that I set myself and whenever I come across an obstacle or an issue I remember earlier or previous challenges and how I overcame them.

By overcoming adversity and pain, came strength and resilience beyond what I ever imagined would be possible.

Surrounding myself with positive like-minded individuals has always had a positive impact. Whether it's people in general or going through the education system or U.W. or business in general, I still find interacting with people who have made a success of themselves, or a situation helps cement my own belief in an opportunity or a system or a product. I have always been a fan of live events and hearing testimonies and speakers helps me maintain a Positive Mental Attitude!

Listening to audio books or reading, in general, is always the best way to keep the mind-expanding; as like a parachute it's better when it's open! Nowadays access to information via the Internet or webinars are a great way of learning.

I always felt that the best approach would be not to let myself become disabled in my mind and make myself believe and dream anything could be possible as long as I feel I can commit to achieving the outcome. Somehow out of all the chaos came clarity!

There is a faithful saying of 'where there's a will there's a way' which is something I firmly believe in, but I also believe, 'where there are wheels there's a way'!

30
HOPES AND DREAMS

I am amazed as I come to the end of this book at how far I have come and what amazing experiences I have felt and places I have been. I never expected for life to turn out so good when I look back to those three months after my injury with nothing to live for.

The main thing I hope for in the future is to maintain this level of health and financial independence and security. There are places I would like to see such as the Grand Canyon and Niagara Falls. I would love to see the Caribbean, Morocco and Hawaii. I would love to find someone to enjoy these experiences with!

I have wanted to do a hot air balloon ride for years so I would love to tick this off too, initially I looked into this and found there is one place in the U.K. that is safe and certified, but the cost was £700 for 2 people, the chances of getting right flying conditions here are very slim. I recently saw a video of a wheelchair travel writer flying over Barcelona for €340 for 2 people, and it looked spectacular!

I would love to have a holiday home somewhere warm with an adapted vehicle and hoist there so I can get away in the winters.

I want people who have listened to my talks and read my books to look at their own lives and be able to overcome obstacles and not just spend a lifetime working to build someone else's dreams. Find your own!

I hope to have broken down some barriers and perceptions of what it is like to live with a disability and what can be achieved when you set your mind to it. You can accomplish so much by challenging yourself, overcoming obstacles and adversity, digging deep into your inner strength when all odds are against you, by letting yourself believe something is possible even though others doubt it.

No one knows what's around the corner and I chose to live this life of possibility, not dwell on my disability, and I will Keep on Rolling!

LIFE ISN'T ABOUT
WAITING FOR
THE STORM TO PASS
IT'S ABOUT LEARNING TO
DANCE IN THE RAIN

Acknowledgements

There are lots of people I would like to thank for helping me get through this journey. My Dad and Gill for always being there for me, with support and financial help, it can't have been easy at the start. My brother and family for all their support throughout the years.
Dawn for sorting out rotas and wages and helping keep a team together for years, considering some of the carers we have had this has been a difficult task. Elk,Jay,Dave and Pro for being the best mates one could possibly have asked for, we have certainly had some laughs over the years. All the carers that have helped me through out the years to maintain a healthy body,Wayne,Andy,Lisa,Dawn,Adam,Kath,Gianni and anyone who has been involved.Sian for giving me the opportunity to get involved with the S.A.N.D. sports club. Adam Barr for introducing me and supporting me with U.W. Tony Leakes for helping me with public speaking. Rik for social media help. Russell for two excellent book covers. Lorna for years of reiki, which have definitely helped keep me healthy.
Jane for help and advise for proofreading. Publishing push for marketing. I am sure there are more but if you have helped me one way or another,then thank you.

48768002R00134

Printed in Poland
by Amazon Fulfillment
Poland Sp. z o.o., Wrocław